WOMEN AND WOMANHOOD
IN THE TALMUD

Program in Judaic Studies
Brown University
BROWN JUDAIC STUDIES

Edited by
Shaye J. D. Cohen

Number 321

WOMEN AND WOMANHOOD IN THE TALMUD

by
Shulamit Valler

WOMEN AND WOMANHOOD
IN THE TALMUD

Shulamit Valler

translated by
Betty Sigler Rozen

foreword by
Judith Hauptman

Brown Judaic Studies
Providence

WOMEN AND WOMANHOOD IN THE TALMUD

by
Shulamit Valler

Copyright © 1999 by Brown University

All rights reserved. No part of this work may be reproduced or transmitted in any form or by any means, electronic or mechanical, including photocopying and recording, or by means of any information storage or retrieval system, except as may be expressly permitted by the 1976 Copyright Act or in writing from Brown Judaic Studies, Brown University, Box 1826, Providence, RI 02912.

Library of Congress Cataloging-in-Publication Data

Valler, Shulamit.
 [Nashim ve-nashiyut be-sipure ha-Talmud. English]
 Women and womanhood in the Talmud / by Shulamit Valler; translated by Betty Sigler Rozen ; foreword by Judith Hauptman.
   p. cm. — (Brown Judaic studies ; no. 321)
 Includes bibliographical references and index.
 ISBN 0-7885-0597-1 (cloth : alk. paper) — ISBN 1-930675-05-4 (pbk. : alk. paper)
 1. Women in rabbinical literature. I. Title. II. Series.

BM509.W7 V3513 1999   99-047020

Printed in the United States of America
on acid-free paper

Table of Contents

Foreword by Judith Hauptman vii

Preface xi

1. Introduction 1
2. How We Dance before the Bride 11
3. The Bride Was Not a Virgin! 29
4. Leaving Home to Study Torah 51
5. Women and Wine 77
6. Mothers and Sons 99

Afterword 121

Bibliography 125

Index of Texts Discussed 131

Index of Names 135

Index of Subjects 137

Foreword

In this short book, a study of five clusters of stories about women, Shulamit Valler makes us see things we would not have seen on our own. Were one simply to read these texts as they appear in the Talmud, the narrative line would be clear, as would certain rabbinic stances toward women, but the reader would not know how each story attained its final form nor how the individual stories coalesced into a collection. And yet it is precisely in these editorial alterations that the deeper message of the text lies.

In bringing these issues to our attention, Valler makes an important contribution to the world of Talmud scholarship. Utilizing the powerful techniques developed to date for reading and analyzing narrative passages, she enters into the mind of the editor who shaped and assembled the discrete units and helps us understand his goals.

It is a standard scholarly assumption that someone who produces a collection of this sort has an agenda of his own and that in the process of creating the collection, he molds the texts in accordance with that agenda. As Valler demonstrates in her close comparative reading of the texts, the editor reworked the old stories in order to have them express his own point of view on matters relating to women. She then shows us that, upon joining the discrete units together into a collection and deliberately establishing linguistic and thematic links among them, the editor took advantage of the opportunity to state his point once again. The whole that he creates is thus greater than the sum of its parts.

As Valler leads us through each collection of texts, she highlights these literary and legal features. Then, upon reading all five clusters of stories in the light of each other, she makes the remarkable observation that in almost all of the anecdotes the rabbinic judge rendered a decision that differed radically from the rule prescribed for just such a case in the immediately preceding Halakhic discussion. It is remarkable that rabbis develop laws and then do not apply them to cases that arise, but it is truly astonishing to learn from Valler that the deviation from the prescribed rule almost always favors women.

If the rabbis, upon examining an issue from a variety of angles, decided, for instance, that a widow did *not* deserve a wine allowance, then the anecdotes that the gemara presents, in conjunction with that Halakhic decision, should arrive at the same conclusion. But, as she shows us, the anecdotes that reflect life as it was lived arrive at the conclusion that such an allowance *should* be made. Similarly, a story about a rabbi who merely gazed at a bride was rewritten by the editor so that he not only looked upon but even danced with her at her wedding.

It is therefore easy to see the importance of this monograph for women's studies. Since most ancient societies were patriarchal, ancient Jewish society as well, the legal bias in favor of men can very easily be noted in the Halakhic texts. However, if all that the untrained reader sees is the bias, and not the accompanying departures from it, then the reading is incomplete and even shallow. Or, if an untrained rear views the stringent halakhah as the essential, prescriptive statement and the conflicting anecdotes as exceptions to the rule, the interpretation is wrong. Studies like Valler's make it clear that to grasp rabbinic attitudes fully and correctly, as they developed over time, one has to read sources in context and together with parallel versions.

Without denying the patriarchal configuration of society, Valler reads the texts her way and arrives at a much more nuanced understanding of the patriarchy. Like some of the contemporary feminist readings of biblical texts, which uncover evidence of counter-traditional voices, Valler's readings of Talmudic case histories elucidate the rabbis' attitudes to women and how these attitudes affected their legislative rulings. A major finding is that as time passes and as laws cross geographical boundaries, adjustments to the law are introduced in practice, even though the statement of the law in principle is left untouched.

A different contribution of this slim volume is its shedding light, if only a little, on women's history. Since the Talmud is peopled by men, many of whom are rabbis, and it is their own life experiences that they draw upon when framing legislation, much less is known about the day-to-day lives of women in that period. But, as social historians have shown, the sources about women and also men must be read in a methodologically sophisticated manner in order to detect historical truths. This may mean, for instance, that the particular rabbi in ancient Israel whom the Talmud Bavli sages say once danced with a bride did not do so, even though it seems rather certain that his Babylonian colleagues, at a later time, did. And that is worth noting and knowing.

Foreword

In short, this book is clear, fascinating, and thought provoking. Each chapter further supports and develops the author's central thesis. By the time one reaches the end, the reader is convinced that the rabbis of the Talmud, and, possibly more important, the editors of the Talmud, began to develop more positive attitudes toward women, their rights, and their privileges.

Judith Hauptman
Jewish Theological Seminary

Preface

A struggle for women's rights and equality between the sexes is a characteristic of the modern world. In the Jewish and in the Israeli world, women's protests against discrimination as practiced today often include protests against ancient Jewish culture, which makes sharp distinctions between the status of men and that of women.

While it is doubtful whether such activities of Jewish and Israeli women have in fact contributed to a change in their social status, it is abundantly clear that they have encouraged the publication of studies on women's rights as expressed in traditional Jewish sources—studies written by both men and women.

This book proposes to examine the viewpoints of the sages of the Mishnah and the Talmud with regard to women and femininity. Hence I begin by surveying the main points made by scholars who have written on the status of women within rabbinic literature.

Most scholars and writers agree that the entire body of rabbinic literature has a male orientation, which clearly distinguishes between men and women. In contrast to this unanimity, scholars disagree on whether the sages of the Mishnaic and Talmudic period *discriminated* against women, or merely *distinguished* between their world and the world of men and, if so, why they made these distinctions.

The answers range from complete apologetics based on the argument that the sages merely adopted and expressed natural differences and role divisions, to a frontal attack on the sages' alleged sense of superiority: they were not acting out of a desire for social justice even when they treated women favorably.

Yehuda Elitzur adopts the apologetic approach when he discusses the place of women in biblical thought.[1] He goes to great lengths to prove that although men and women in the Bible are of equal value, they

---

[1] Yehuda Elitzur, "Women in Biblical Thought," in *Hagut:* A Collection of Essays on Jewish Thought (Jerusalem, 1983) (Hebrew). The article also appeared in *HaPeninah* (Jerusalem, 1989).

cannot fulfill equal roles because this would be an equality like that achieved, according to the Aggadah, by the inhabitants of Sodom, who shortened or stretched everyone to fit the length of their bed. According to Elitzur, one aim of Genesis is to teach that the correct sexual equality is that expressed by the division of sex roles. He explains that rabbinic law, under which leadership tasks are allotted specifically to men, may have developed from the sex divisions in the Bible.

It is difficult to accept Elitzur's view that biblical law accords men and women equal status when we consider the biblical laws concerning rape and suspected adultery, or that a young girl is to be stoned to death if found not to be a virgin when she marries. Even the law from Deuteronomy 22:22 cited to prove how liberal the Torah is—"If a man is found lying with a married woman, they shall both die"—has a strong flavor of inequality.[2] But since we are not dealing with the Bible, we confine ourselves to Elitzur's explanation as to how discrimination against women in the Talmudic period began. According to him it was the natural (and therefore just) division of roles that caused the rabbis to prevent women from participating as equals in social life.

Elitzur's approach finds expression in the writings of other Orthodox rabbis and scholars[3] who make every effort to prove that the rabbis of the Talmud respected men and women as equals. They argue, however, that there was a just and natural distinction between the roles of the sexes and hence between the social status of and the tasks undertaken by each group.

Ileana Amado Levi[4] goes even further when she claims that although Jewish culture was of necessity influenced by the school of thought prevailing in neighboring cultures that emphasized male centrality, it was the only one to give real answers to women's problems: (1) because Jewish culture, aware of its imperfections, is in a constant state of dynamic change and (2) because Jewish law does not isolate the problem of women's status but places it in the context of the problematic relationship between the sexes, to be solved in the course of history.

---

[2]Against his argument that this is a more enlightened approach than the one expressed in Hammurabi's Code, where the husband is the master and decides what to do with the wife, examples from Babylonian codes also show that women owned property, performed judicial acts, made contracts, and inherited part of their husbands' property; and from Egyptian codes in which men and women enjoyed equal status. See Blu Greenberg, *On Women and Judaism*, chap. 4 (Philadelphia, 1981).
[3]See, for example, Rabbi Nahum Draizin, "The Status and Education of Women in the Halakhah," *Or Ha-Mizrah* 16 (1967) (Hebrew).
[4]Ileana Amado Levi Valensi, "Cultures and Their Relationship to the Status of Women," *Prooftext* 10, 62.

According to her, the exclusion of women from certain areas of Judaism is based on biological facts. It is the natural bondage of the female that has led the male to make history, but he has done such a bad job that he has no cause for pride or joy.

Amado Levi analyzes the subject philosophically and does not attempt to give explanations on the level of the real world. Even philosophically, however, this viewpoint can be refuted, for it is hard to agree that not making history is a virtue. It is equally difficult to agree with the biological argument, for it was precisely in Jewish society where the ability to bear children is so important that it should have been considered an advantage, giving women a superior social position.

Cynthia Ozick[5] strongly attacks the biological argument as a justification of the role division, and as an explanation for women's inferior position. She considers the division between masculine and feminine roles, and even the laws laid down by the rabbis to redress legal injustice to women, deeply insulting. According to Ozick, the laws introduced to improve the situation of women did not spring from a sense of justice, but were an act of charity by the strong for the weak. She cites cases in which Jewish law took a strong stand against injustices created by nature, like the commandment to rest during Sabbath or the commandment to honor father and mother, and expresses surprise that there is no law in the Torah against diminishing a woman's humanity. Neither did the Jewish Oral Law, generally able to devise new statutes, create a necessary law such as this. Beyond the question of whether the natural division of roles expresses justice and equality, as Elitzur asserts, or is an insult, as claimed by Ozick, it is difficult to explain the whole corpus of laws concerning women's status in the Talmudic period on the basis of nature alone.

Eliezer Berkovitz's approach is different and deeper.[6] He distinguishes between the ethical aspects of women's status, in which he claims that the wife's status in the Jewish family throughout the generations was more important and more central than in any other culture in which Jews lived, and the social aspects, in which equality was totally absent. Berkovitz points out that on the legal level the rabbis made serious efforts to correct injustices whose source lay in the Bible, and to make the wife's family rights equal to those of the husband, which proves that the rabbis were aware of that injustice. He admits, however, that on the social level the situation was totally different, and that there is

---

[5]Cynthia Ozick, "Observations on How to Find the Right Question," in *HaPeninah* (Jerusalem, 1989).
[6]Eliezer Berkovitz, "The Position of Women in Judaism: The Socio-Halakhic Aspect," in *Hagut* (Jerusalem, 1983) (Hebrew).

no doubt that this situation stemmed from a male attitude to the nature of women—an attitude which, according to Berkovitz, was not based on the Torah.

The distinction between the biblical and Talmudic periods as to the male view of the female sex, and the social status of women, is noted and substantiated by Theodore Friedman.[7] His evidence shows that during biblical times, women participated in religious and ceremonial activities. There were female prophets, there were female diplomats, and apart from the priestly service, there was in practice no area of public life from which women were barred. By contrast, in Talmudic times women were not given communal or religious roles. A woman's main task was to tend the home and bear children, and according to the Amora Rav Dimi, in the Babylonian Talmud (Eruvin 100b): "She is wrapped up like a mourner, banished from the company of all men, and confined within a prison."

Though Friedman distinguishes clearly between the attitude toward women in the biblical and Talmudic periods, he too does not argue that women were discriminated against economically or within the family. His quotations are mostly evidence of social discrimination alone. It seems, therefore, that he would surely agree with the distinction drawn by Eliezer Berkovitz.[8]

Ya'akov Elbaum analyzes women's status in the Talmudic period from another angle.[9] He considers the *opinions* of the rabbis rather than their *legislation* on the position and nature of women. He makes a distinction between sayings and indirect insights on one hand, and Halakhic rulings on the other. After an attempt to understand the rabbis' attitude toward women, as expressed by their direct and indirect statements in Aggadic literature, he concludes that despite the difficulties caused by variant readings in establishing the original texts, it is clear that rabbinic literature, while expressing both positive and negative attitudes toward women, was written with a masculine orientation. He believes that the masculine attitude reflected in sayings and stories may well also represent Halakhic attitudes.

In summary, despite the different distinctions they draw, all the scholars cited above agree that all branches of rabbinic literature were written from a masculine viewpoint. The female sex is considered weak and naturally predestined to fulfill functions and roles different from

---

[7] Theodore Friedman, "The Shifting Role of Women from the Bible to the Talmud," *Judaism* 36, no. 4 (1987).
[8] A similar distinction on the status of women in the Halakhah is made in Ann Lapidus Lerner's *Who Hast Not Made Me a Man*.
[9] Ya'akov Elbaum, "Female Characters in Aggadic Literature: A Model for Imitation," in *Hagut* (Jerusalem, 1983) (Hebrew).

Preface xv

those of males. Attempts to treat women justly reflected the desire of the strong to be just to the weak. Although the rabbis' attitude toward women was respectful, recognizing and appreciating their good qualities and their important role in home and family, the picture rabbinic literature provides as a whole is not one of two separate but equal sectors of the population, but rather of a strong, dominant, and active group that at best expresses consideration for the second group's weakness and passivity.

To reinforce my previous remarks I provide the following passages from a collection of sayings and stories in the Babylonian Talmud[10] which praise women. I have deliberately chosen sayings that enumerate women's fine qualities in order to show just how overwhelming the male orientation of the rabbis is.

First, two statements by Rabbi Eleazar expressing the profound importance of the woman for the man:

> Rabbi Eleazar said: Any man who has no wife is no man, for it is said: "Male and female created He them and He called their name man." Rabbi Eleazar also said: What is the meaning of the biblical verse, "I will make him a help meet for him?" If he is worthy, she is a help to him. If he is not worthy, she is against him. And others say: Rabbi Eleazar pointed out a contradiction. It is written kenegedo [meaning 'to strike'], but we can read it as *kenegedo* [meaning 'meet for him']! If he is *worthy*, she is 'meet for him'. If he is *not worthy*, she chastises him.

Finally, the story of Rabbi Hiyya also reflects an approach in which the role of woman is limited to providing for the needs of the man:

> Rabbi Hiyya was constantly tormented by his wife. But whenever he found something suitable he would wrap it in his scarf and bring it to her. Rav said to him: "But surely she is tormenting you." "Sir," he replied to him, "it is sufficient for us that they rear *our children* and deliver *us* from sin."

The passage above is clearly male-oriented, expressing a certain contempt for the female sex. It certainly does not express the equality claimed by Professor Elitzur.

What gave rise to this male-oriented approach to the female sex and what is the background to its development?

In my opinion, the superficial answer that it is no more than an expression of the natural division of gender roles should be totally rejected. The problem is not the division of gender roles itself, but the way society views those roles. The sentence the Babylonian Talmud ascribes to Elijah—"If a man brings wheat, does he chew wheat? If flax,

---

[10]Babylonian Talmud, Yevamot 63a-63b.

does he wear flax?"[11]—might well have expressed an egalitarian idea regarding a fair division of roles, had it not been for the opening and concluding sentences to which it is connected. The introduction to this passage points out that it was a reply to Rabbi Jose's question: "How does a woman help a *man*?" And the conclusion takes the form of a rhetorical question: "Does she not, then bring light to *his eyes* and set him on *his feet*?" The division of roles is not a division between equals. The sole purpose of the woman's role is to help the man stand on his feet and bring light to his eyes.

In addition, the natural explanation does not say why women were barred from religious rites and ceremonies, why their appearance in legal proceedings was considered unseemly, why they were prevented from "speaking with all men," why "beauty" and "children" were considered the exclusive purposes of their existence, and why they were considered intellectually inferior, condemned to segregation from the world of men in the isolation of their homes.[12]

Moreover, how did it happen that "and ye shall teach them to your children" (Deuteronomy 11:19) was interpreted as a commandment to teach Torah only to boys (Kidushin 29b)? What was the social and cultural background to such an interpretation?

Theodore Friedman claims[13] that every constituent part of women's status in the Talmud is paralleled in Athenian society of the post-Homeric period. (He considers Sparta an exception, because it practiced full equality of the sexes.) Friedman demonstrates through abundant quotations from the Greek dramatists that the Athenian woman was isolated and shut away in her home, and even there her contact with male society was kept to a minimum. Quoting Plato and Aristotle, he shows that women had an inferior status spiritually, were not educated beyond training in domestic tasks, and were destined to bear children and look after their husbands' domestic needs.

Friedman concludes that the broad influence of Greek culture on Jewish culture makes it likely that Judaism was influenced in this area too, and that the discrimination against women in the Mishnaic and Talmudic periods was no more than an import from Athens.[14]

---

[11] Babylonian Talmud, Yevamot 63a.
[12] Ozick, "Observations."
[13] "Shifting Role of Women."
[14] Dreizin makes a similar point, "Status and Education of Women." According to him, "those who spoke contemptuously of women were influenced by foreign ideas and customs." He cites examples from Philo.

A.A. Halevi's book *Aggadic and Halakhic Values in the Light of Greek and Latin Sources*[15] offers many parallels between Greek and rabbinic sayings and laws pertaining to women. Among the Greek sayings he cites are those that present women as frivolous sexual objects (whose sexuality is albeit concealed) and for whom only the confines of the home are appropriate. Halevi's long list of quotations makes it reasonable to conclude that the duality of the rabbis toward women derived from Greek culture. Both in Greek and Roman sources we find, on one hand, great appreciation for women and for their role in marriage, and high regard for marriage and love in general, and, on the other hand, the conviction that men are the rulers and the expectation that their wives should obey them. Halevi's work also reveals a great similarity between rabbinic and Greco-Roman legislation.

It therefore seems a reasonable assumption that the rabbis' attitude toward the female sex was influenced by their cultural surroundings and in particular by Greek culture. However, this still does not explain fully the gap between Jewish women's status in the biblical and the Talmudic periods, and specifically, why their legal position improved but their social position deteriorated.

Tal Ilan in *Jewish Women in Greco-Roman Times*[16] reviews the articles and books published in the last two hundred years on women's status in Jewish society. She quotes scholars who explain the change in women's status in Jewish society between Bible times and the period of the Mishnah and the Talmud in various ways. However, she herself concludes that there is not a single historical study among them that investigates rabbinic sources critically, which would help make it possible to explain the change.

Some scholars that Ilan cites attribute this change in women's status in Jewish society to the influence of Christianity. They maintain that in the classical world, particularly in Sparta but in Athens too, women enjoyed freedom and liberal attitudes flourished, and that only later, under Christian influence (or as some researchers maintain, under Jewish influence that returned through Christianity) did their situation change. Thus C. Seltman (Cambridge, MA, 1956) and A. Hecker (Cambridge, MA, 1970). If we agree that the situation of the Jewish woman worsened under the influence of Christianity, we then must ask ourselves whether ancient Judaism influenced Christianity to adopt a less sympathetic attitude toward women, or vice versa.

---

[15] A.A. Halevi, *Aggadic and Halakhic Values in the Light of Greek and Latin Sources*, vol. 4 (Tel Aviv, 1980), pp. 198-309 (Hebrew).
[16] Tal Ilan, *Jewish Women in Greco-Roman Times* (Tübingen, 1995).

D. Boyarin considers this question in *Carnal Israel*,[17] and denies that Christianity influenced Judaism or that Judaism influenced Christianity, and indeed that women's status deteriorated in Talmudic times at all: Boyarin maintains that the attitude of ancient Judaism to women was more sympathetic than that of Christianity or of Greek culture which preceded Christianity. He does find rabbinic literature asymmetric in its portrayal of the two sexes, women being considered as a means to satisfy men's sexual and reproductive needs. Nonetheless, this involves no demonization of women, and marriage and sexuality are considered positive, as opposed to the prevailing attitude among the Hellenists and their Christian heirs.

Reinforcing what he has said about the Sages' positive attitude toward women, Boyarin examines their literature according to the distinction made by Sherry Ortner (1974). Here there are three versions of female inferiority in different cultures: 1) ideological elements and declarations that reduce the value of women; 2) the use of words that emphasize women's inferiority; 3) prestigious social institutions in which women may not participate.

Boyarin maintains that neither the first nor the second version exists in rabbinic literature. As to the third, he distinguishes between Jewish society in Palestine and that in Babylonia. In my opinion he is quite wrong about the first two versions. I have quoted numerous expressions, including those that appear to flatter women, while clearly detracting from their worth. Even his third version does not serve as a counterweight to the social inferiority of women in Talmudic literature. I agree entirely with Tal Ilan: she considers Boyarin mistaken in confusing positive attitudes in Judaism toward marriage and sexuality with its attitudes toward women.

A different explanation for the change in women's status in Jewish society is found in Neusner's commentary on the Mishnah Tractate Nashim, later developed by his student Judith Wegner in *The Status of Women in the Mishnah*.[18] From their understanding it follows that women's social status indeed deteriorated in the period in question because of the structure and, even more, because of the ideology on which Jewish society was based at that time.

Jewish society had been a temple society and its central ideology was one of purity. The periodic changes arising from female physiology appeared to threaten the purity and spirituality of men. Men's fears led them to want to subordinate women in everything concerned with their sexuality and reproductive powers.

---

[17] Daniel Boyarin, *Carnal Israel* (Berkeley, 1993).
[18] Judith Wegner, *The Status of Women in the Mishnah* (New York, 1988).

Preface

Boyarin also links women's exclusion from the intellectual sphere, and from prestigious social institutions, with male fears of their sexuality. However, he does not discuss Mishnaic times, and does not base his statements on the nature of a temple society. His book deals with the Talmudic period and with differences between Jewish society in Palestine and Babylon. According to him, in Palestine women studying Torah was a realistic possibility, while in Babylon the prevailing attitude was that an intellectually or politically active woman was one who had thrown off sexual restraints.

In his view, the Babylonian conception developed as a kind of male line of defense. Men's power in the world gave them a superiority that compensated them for women's reproductive superiority, and at the same time guaranteed that the latter process would continue. But Boyarin does not explain why this concept developed in Babylonia rather than elsewhere, nor how he arrived at the conclusion, despite his view that the position of women in Jewish society did not deteriorate in Talmudic times.

From what Neusner, Wegner, and Boyarin have written, it may be possible to derive a satisfactory answer to the question of why the status of women in Jewish society changed during the Mishnaic and Talmudic periods.

We base the explanation we are about to present on the work of the sociologist Yael Atzmon, in her article "Judaism and the Removal of Women from Society."[19] There she maintains that reasons for keeping women out of public life should be sought in the society's power balance and in the interest of the social regime.

On the basis of the ideological and structural nature of Jewish society in Mishnaic times, then, and given male anxieties relating to female sexuality and superiority in the reproductive process, the change in women's status in this period can be explained.

The transition from biblical society with its firmly established social institutions, to that of the Mishnah, where the powers of the Sages and intellectuals were not clearly defined, naturally made this ruling class suspicious of every attempt against the social order so lately constructed, and with such great effort.

The association of women with physicality and with changing bodily conditions may have been perceived to threaten both bodily purity so central during the Temple period, and the intellectuality that became central after the destruction. It is reasonable to assume, too, that female

---

[19] Yael Atzmon, "Judaism and the Removal of Women from Society," in *A View into Lives of Women in Jewish Societies*, ed. Yael Atzmon (Jerusalem, 1995) (Hebrew).

control in reproduction was also perceived to threaten the social order at a time when there were rapid changes in the power balance between different groups, and traditional regulatory arrangements had been undermined or suspended.

In conclusion, it is possible that changes in the structure of society and of power during Mishnaic and Talmudic times led men to strengthen their position in spiritual and intellectual areas and in the institutions of power based on them. Hence men made efforts to push women out of intellectual life and out of the institutions wherein the ruling elite was created. From this assumption we move on to this book's specific topic—an attempt to reveal the undeclared view of the scholars of the Mishnah and the Talmud on the nature of the female sex and women's thoughts and feelings. We ask whether there is a difference between the view-points expressed openly in laws and Aggadot and the rabbis' concealed thought world, which reveals itself only in hints between the lines.

1

Introduction

1. The Method

In "Female Characters in Aggadic Literature: A Model for Imitation,"[1] Ya'akov Elbaum has this to say about rabbinic literature:

> It seems to me that it is precisely in the seemingly indirect references—in the descriptions of biblical personalities, and also in the stories about contemporary women and their place in society—that we find more significant indications [of rabbis' attitudes toward women] than those in statements that deal directly with the subject.

This quotation expresses the methodological premise on which this book is based.

The basic assumption of this study is that it would not be correct to establish the characteristics of the rabbinic attitude toward women on the personal and social level from the regulations the rabbis promulgated, the laws they passed, or the positions they expressed in stories and sayings.

The Sages expressed themselves on both legal and moral levels in keeping with the culture of their times. In addition, such values as family unity, begetting children, and concern for and care of the next generation were central ideals in the world of the rabbis. Since these values were linked to protecting and preserving the image and the traditional roles of women, it is unreasonable to expect the rabbis to have legislated openly and innovatively on behalf of women's social and public equality, and it

---

[1]Ya'akov Elbaum, "Female characters in Aggadic literature: A Model for Imitation," in *Hagut* (Jerusalem, 1983) (Hebrew).

is similarly unreasonable to expect expressions of opinion by women on these subjects.[2]

We do find a well-known statement in Yalkut Shimoni, Shofetim 1: "I call heaven and earth to witness that whether Jew or non-Jew, *whether man or woman,* whether slave or maidservant, it is all in accordance with man's deeds that the holy spirit rests upon him." However, this is an unusual statement with few parallels, uttered in response to the extreme viewpoint of the Amora Rabbi Berekhah: "Woe to the generation that has a woman as its leader."

To understand the rabbinic attitude toward women and femininity, we must look for descriptions and stories that hint at it between the lines. I have thus tried to find material in which I can trace such hints, and to investigate whether an understanding of and sensitivity to the rational and emotional world of women can be found in the words of the rabbis, and whether this material testifies to an attitude in which women are treated as men's equals.

I have limited my search to collections of stories in the Babylonian Talmud. By examining them, I have discovered approaches and attitudes stated in the most indirect ways. Even an attitude expressed in an Aggadic story, or in the way a female biblical character is depicted, has a degree of directness about it. However, the way in which the collections of stories were edited contains the most oblique and concealed, yet significant, hints of attitudes and approaches. These hints are sometimes conveyed in the role of the editor in formulating the individual stories, and sometimes by the way the stories are arranged and the collection structured. I have investigated five such collections, four from the tractate Ketubot and one from the tractate Kidushin.

I have first examined the individual stories as they appear in the Babylonian Talmud, then compared them to parallels in the Jerusalem Talmud and in the Midrashim. I have also compared the text of the Venice edition with manuscript versions and with other printed editions.

It was thus possible to discover how stories in the Babylonian Talmud were fashioned stylistically in order to make them fit into their place and role in the collections of which they became a part. Once the construction, editing, and organization of the stories became clear, the

---

[2]The women who take part in philosophical or ideological debates in the Talmud are either non-Jews or Jewish women engaged in debates with them. Such incidents are mentioned in Sanhedrin 4b and 38b. Women usually appear in the Talmud in practical matters connected with the home and family, childbirth, raising children, and medical matters, where their expertise derives from their practical roles. Such incidents are mentioned in Mo'ed Katan 28b, Shabbat 133b, Pesahim 106a, and elsewhere.

Introduction

motives of the editors and their positions on a wide variety of subjects related to women's status and femininity emerged.

2. The Literary Editing of the Babylonian Talmud

Two basic principles guide my search for indirect expression of perceptions of and attitudes toward women in the stories of the Babylonian Talmud:

a. The collections of stories we have before us in the Talmud contain authentic nuclear material that has been worked over and edited.
b. This reworking and editing has been done in the service of specific attitudes and approaches.

In justification of these assumptions, I point out that

1. the Babylonian Talmud is a literary work that has undergone literary editing;
2. a common result of editing is the emergence of collections;
3. numerous collections in the Babylonian Talmud are based on kernel stories (sometimes earlier material from Palestine) reworked and adapted to the new contexts in which they were placed.

Before going into these matters, a short explanation of the terms 'Talmud' and 'Babylonian Talmud' is in order.

The basis of both *Talmuds* is the *Mishnah*.

The Mishnah is a compilation according to subjects of all the Halakhic material of the Oral Law created in Palestine up to the end of the second century C.E. The editor of the Mishnah—Rabbi Judah Ha-nasi—left for the generations to come a complete and ordered work to be studied and interpreted.

From the early third century, the Sages in Palestine and Babylonia, the Amoraim, occupied themselves with interpreting the Mishnah. Their labors continued for some 400 years, eventually producing the *Jerusalem Talmud* and the *Babylonian Talmud*.

The Amoraim interpreted the Mishnah first of all through *beraitot*, Tannaitic fragments not included by Rabbi Judah Ha-nasi in his Mishnah, but which, because they were often ordered and detailed, could help in the understanding of that book. However, the Amoraim also produced their own interpretive literature. Hence both Talmuds contain sayings, problems, and judgments the Amoraim made on cases brought before them, as well as stories and homiletic commentaries.

Neither Talmud provides information as to how it came into being nor about its editorial process, and so we can surmise the history of the texts only from the Halakhic and literary material before us.

As to the Babylonian Talmud, the focus of our attention, all scholars agree that it does not contain simply a record of what the Amoraim actually said.

Some think that there was a single, comprehensive editing of the material. Others, however, think that the Babylonian Talmud is not the result of a single editorial initiative but rather of a lengthy creative process that included editing and literary enhancement of the discussions.

All agree, however, that the discussions, i.e., the subject-oriented units of deliberation, are the result of the reworking and editing of previous materials by the Amoraim, based on the Mishnah and the beraitot. Editorial work is recognized especially in the "filler" between the sayings of the Amoraim—in the questions, explanations, and standard terms presented anonymously, which are hence called "*stam* Talmud" (anonymous Talmud).

Our concern here is not to delve into signals that indicate the different times and trends during which editing was carried out. It suffices to cite Professor Shama Friedman who notes three different elements in Babylonian Talmud discussions, apart from mishnayot and beraitot: a) sayings of the Amoraim, b) *stam* Talmud, c) later additions (from the introduction to his book פרק האישה רבה בבבלי, which is a general introduction to methods for studying the Talmud). For the purposes of this book, a study of story collections, it is important to distinguish between authentic material—the words of the Amoraim (and sometimes the Tannaim who preceded them)—and the editing involved in the *stam*, which may be expressed in words and phrases that are a sort of editorial comment, or in the arrangement of the elements in the collection, which serves the same purpose.

Less important is the distinction between layers of editing, that is, between *stam* Talmud and later additions. (Friedman cites a few instances of scholars who stressed differences between the sayings of the Amoraim and the *stam*, and he himself writes that this is a significant distinction for purposes of interpretation.) For our purpose, however, the important distinction is between authentic material and the editorial layer in the story collections.

Here for the most part I use the research of Abraham Weiss on the collection as a literary form in the Babylonian Talmud. In *The Literary Works of the Amoraim*[3] Weiss speaks of "the collection as a literary form of arranging traditional material." He explains also that such collections

---

[3] Abraham Weiss, *The Literary Creation of the Amoraim* (New York, 1962), pp. 176-231 (Hebrew).

already appear in Tannaitic literature, where statements and laws have been brought together to "form a unit with its own internal framework."

Weiss points out that the organizational framework of the Tannaitic collections is sometimes practical, sometimes formal, and sometimes personal (the name of the rabbi who wrote or transmitted the statements). On the other hand, the problem of how the parts of such collections fit together is connected to the general question of how Talmudic material was organized. On this point, in *On the Talmud*[4] Weiss writes that "the creation of the Talmud...was a long process of literary decisions in which one layer was added to the other." And in *The Creation of the Talmud in Its Entirety*,[5] he explains that scholars of later generations received explanations and clarifications of the Mishnayot. Some of this material was already in an established literary form, whereas some was not. The rabbis "placed these explanations next to each other, completed some on the basis of others, and molded them all together into a literary unity linked by context."

In his book on the literary work of the Amoraim,[6] Weiss assembles many examples of collections spoken or transmitted at one time. These he contrasts with other collections that emerged with an organizational framework established by the editor. Among the latter, he cites examples in which the individual statements are the words of one author, or one rabbi transmitting them in the name of another—statements made on different occasions and for some reason assembled later. He also gives examples of collections containing different layers of source material, and others that took on their present expanded form due to the inclusion of additional statements.

Weiss's examples make it abundantly clear that Amoraic literature contains collections composed of different layers of source material, organized and edited later, and that they are not the result of grouping statements by one rabbi into independent source units. These collections clearly demonstrate a widespread tendency to organize material on the basis of common interest and to move from one subject to another within a common thematic framework.

After examining all the collections connected with women in the tractates of Seder Nashim in the Babylonian Talmud, I decided to look more closely at five story collections that were clearly not edited in accordance with any formal criterion. The stories there were not discussed before or told by one particular rabbi. Some are linked directly

---

[4] Abraham Weiss, *A Study of the Talmud*, (New York, 1943), p. 107 (Hebrew).
[5] Abraham Weiss, *The Creation of the Talmud in Its Entirety* (New York, 1955), pp. 1-56 (Hebrew).
[6] Weiss, *The Literary Creation of the Amoraim*, p. 220ff.

with a Mishnah that forms their starting point, or to the discussion of a related subject, and others are completely devoid of such connections.

From the names of the Tannaim or Amoraim appearing as judges in the stories, clearly the collections under discussion are made up of various layers in the development of the Talmud. Sources brought in from elsewhere are also evident. The stories do not appear to have been put together randomly but rather to have undergone organization, and as they appear before us, they are the result of careful editing. We can identify both kinds of editing of which Weiss speaks:[7]

> The first involves "literary decisions," i.e. stylistic and linguistic editing of each story separately, to establish uniformity in style and expression in the stories as a group. The second is "organizational activity," i.e. placing the stories in a certain order. In the latter groups the collections reveal another interesting phenomenon: in each sub-collection of two or three stories, a common factor and a deliberate arrangement can be identified.

It became necessary then to examine the purpose of the editing and arrangement in order to reveal the viewpoints behind them. My examination revealed three collections that clearly express profeminine views, or at least views considerate toward and sensitive to the way women think, although they do not conform to, or perhaps even oppose, the laws and discussions to which they are linked. Two other collections also express understanding of and sensitivity to women's inclinations and spiritual needs, even though they do not express definite feminist positions that oppose those of Halakhah.

In the next chapters I will deal with each collection individually, examining individual stories and comparing them to parallels elsewhere in the Talmud. This will accentuate the stylistic editing they received, which fit them into their place and role in the collection. I will also justify the underlying thesis of this work by exposing the rationale upon which the organization of the stories is based.

3. The Stories as Presented Here

Of the five collections selected, three deal with unusual events that are crises in women's lives, and the other two with states that are of long-term duration. All deal with subjects, problems, or situations in which women are involved because they live in a world controlled by men.

That the men who appear in the collection as judges can break out of the male-centered thought pattern and understand the feminine position or viewpoint behind the events is impressive indeed. But even more

---

[7] Weiss, *A Study of the Talmud*, pp. 64-66.

Introduction

impressive is how the collections have been edited, clearly showing an editorial point of view.

In the following chapters I deal with the collections in the order in which their themes might occur in a woman's life as bride, wife, and mother. The first three chapters discuss collections relating to unique events or crises.

Chapter 2 analyzes the collections on "How we dance before the bride." The marriage celebration is without doubt a critical event for any young person, male or female. But here attention is focused on the bride alone. Is it mere chance that the words of encouragement and compliments gathered and organized in this collection are directed specifically to the bride? That seems unlikely. Rather it is an expression of deep sensitivity to the fears and hesitations of the young woman facing a new world, new challenges, and an unaccustomed appearance in public. These stories about rabbis who danced before brides reveal that they felt the need to encourage and give pleasure to brides, which even justified breaking down the customary boundaries between the sexes. The thought that the bride in particular needs an unusual degree of encouragement testifies to a rational and emotional ability to overcome a masculine orientation and see the marriage ceremony from the woman's point of view.

Chapter 3 discusses a collection dealing with the husband's claim that his wife was not a virgin when he married her. In the ancient world, the bride's virginity was most important in building and maintaining married life. The possibility of claiming that one's bride was not a virgin on her wedding night gave the husband power, and menaced the wife. A woman whose husband claimed that she was not a virgin was in a most difficult situation. Where the wife was able to refute the charge, it is reasonable to assume that the act of refutation was a source of severe embarrassment to her, and in those cases where she could not, she could expect that her marriage would be dissolved and she would be disgraced.

Add to all this the young woman's confusion and fears regarding the social and economic problems in store for her should her husband's charge not be refuted, and we sense yet more clearly her emotional tension and helplessness. According to Halakhah, if the husband's charge can neither be proved or disproved (details are given later), the court accepts his allegation, because his purpose in appearing before the court was to render his wife forbidden to him. This ruling is based on a clearly male-oriented worldview that a husband who seeks to break the marriage bond by claiming that his wife is not a virgin is doing himself damage in that he is preventing himself from enjoying his wife. She is in an inferior position, because she cannot refute her husband's words even though she may know that they are false.

The collection of stories on the claims of nonvirginity adopts a position quite different from and even opposed to the Halakhic one. Both the individual stories and their organization in the collection express a tendency to understand the wife's situation. Her difficult position is appreciated, and the whole collection testifies to an ability to see things from a woman's perspective, one ignored by the Halakhic lawmakers.

Chapter 4 discusses scholars who leave their homes for extended periods to study Torah. The problem around which these stories are woven is familiar. Even today society expects women to make material and emotional concessions to advance the career, prestige, or spiritual life of their husbands. Even today the problem of leaving home, or the world of the home, for success in another sphere exists, especially in the cases of successful, gifted men motivated by ambition or idealism, like those rabbis who are the protagonists of the Talmudic stories.

Yet in the collection devoted to rabbis who left their homes we find highly developed sensitivity to the feelings and situations of the wives. The feminine point of view finds expression not only in each individual story, but also in the way the stories are edited. The collection is clearly designed to convey the message that mutual understanding, a spirit of partnership and consideration for the wife's wishes and needs are more important than the husband's advance in Torah study, despite its importance and centrality in the Jewish world.

Chapters 5 and 6 analyze collections whose subjects are other than special events or times of crisis. Chapter 5 deals with women and wine. The protagonists of the stories are women living apart from their husbands, who appeal to the court for a wine allowance besides the customary maintenance. An examination of the Talmudic discussion to which this collection is linked shows a tendency to prevent the wife of an absent husband from drinking wine, which was considered likely to lead her into sexual promiscuity. This indicates a patronizing attitude of masculine superiority, and is rejected. Both the individual stories and the complete collection tend to regard the wife's wine allowance as an economic right, and reject the earlier connection between that allowance and sexual behavior. Presenting the wine allowance as part of general maintenance does not, of course, eliminate the wife's dependence on her husband. Still, the rabbis could not be expected to have made such sweeping changes in the wife's economic and legal status, thereby shaking the entire social structure. Regarding the wine allowance as an economic matter alleviates somewhat the insulting tone that accompanies the Halakhic discussion of it. Hence this collection too evidences an understanding of the feminine point of view.

Introduction

Chapter 6 discusses a collection of stories about mothers and sons. In contrast to the stories discussed earlier, it does not reveal women's problems but describes characteristics of female behavior in the context of the complex, lifelong relationship between mothers and sons.

Both the sensitive behavioral patterns set forth in the individual stories and the nuances of the entire collection gradually take us forward through degrees of complexity in this relationship, indicating an impressive ability to penetrate women's inner souls and private thoughts. Such understanding and sensitivity shown by men and expressed in a male-oriented literary work indicates creative and interpretive skills in capturing and appreciating female behavior and thinking.

2

How We Dance before the Bride
(Babylonian Talmud, Ketubot 16b-17a)

Many cultures bless their brides and grooms, singing their praises at the wedding celebration.[1] Among Jews, from the time of the Talmud to the present day, there is an entire series of benedictions, on each of the seven days of celebration that follow the wedding ceremony. The formula is laid down in the Babylonian Talmud (Ketubot 7b-8a) and the focus is the couple, as thanks are rendered to God in joy for the blessings of conjugality. The basis for this is in the Torah where the benediction is directed specifically to Rebecca the bride, by her family:[2] "Thou art our sister, be thou the mother of thousands of millions, and let thy seed possess the gate of those which hate them" (Genesis 24:60). Another biblical blessing that relates to the wife, although addressed to the husband, is the blessing of Boaz, who redeemed Ruth from her childless widowhood: "The Lord make the woman who is coming into thine house like Rachel and like Leah, which two did build the house of Israel; and do thou worthily in Ephratah and be famous in Bethlehem" (Ruth 4:11). The importance of blessing the bride specifically is mentioned in the Mishnah, Tractate Kallah, chap. 1 (Higger edition, p. 169) which states, "A bride unblessed is forbidden as one in her period."

In the Babylonian Talmud, then, in the text above, Rav Judah gives a formula for the bridegroom's blessing, whose theme is both bride and groom. In the same tractate, however, in the text that heads our chapter, there is a hymn of praise sung at wedding celebrations in ancient Israel

---

[1]Edward Westermark, *The History of Human Marriage*, vol. 2. *Hebrew Encyclopedia*, s.v. "hatunah."
[2]Azriel Hildesheimer, "Toldot Berachot Erusim ve-Nesuim" *Sinai*, 10, pp. 107-119.

whose theme was specifically the bride. The passage also includes stories about rabbis who danced before brides.

A.A. Halevi in *Aggadic and Halakhic Values in the Light of Greek and Latin Sources* (pp. 222-223) mentions the ancient Greek custom of playing instruments, singing, and dancing before brides. He quotes from Homer:

> He pictures, then, two cities, noble scenes;
> weddings in one and wedding feasts and brides
> led out through the town by torchlight from their chambers
> amid chorales, amid the young men turning
> round and round in dances: flutes and harps among them,
> keeping up a tune, and women
> coming outdoors to stare as they went by.
> (Iliad 18, 490-496)

He quotes Antigone's lament that she is to be executed in the flower of her youth: "None have sung me wedding songs" (Antigone 813), and Lucretius's lament for Iphigenia: "Not the sacred custom of a wedding in her youth / Not the joyful songs of Hymen..." (1:96).[3]

However, the Greek sources do not tell us the content of the wedding songs. Did they focus on the bride alone or were they, like the blessings in the Talmud, about both partners and the joys of marital life in general?

The hymn of praise to the bride cited in Ketubot (16b-17a), however, is for the bride only, and the rabbis dance before her and with her, their sole purpose to make her happy.

Unlike similar customs in other cultures, or in the Bible, these dances have nothing to do with warding off dangers or assuring fertility.[4] They do not even express gratitude for the blessings of conjugal life, like the Seven Benedictions of the Talmud. The sole theme of the hymns is to praise the bride's beauty and her virtue, as the sole purpose of the dance is her entertainment and happiness. The program, as it were, is for the bride and not for the couple, to allay uneasiness and to bring her joy and heart's ease.

From the collection cited in Ketubot, the songs sung to the bride at her wedding appear to have resembled those sung to men at receptions in their honor. The use of the same song for brides and for distinguished men indicates that the center of wedding celebrations was the bride. All eyes were on her. From the collection of stories on Eretz Israel Sages who danced before or with brides, as indicated in the discussion in Ketubot, it is quite clear that it was totally out of keeping with their conduct on

---

[3]Hymaneus (like Hinoma in the Mishnah) is merely the Greek wedding ceremony and, by extension this is a wedding song.
[4]Westermark, *The History of Human Marriage*, pp. 496-595.

other occasions. The astonishment of the other sages at what they then beheld is conveyed further on, in responses stating that the customary dignified deportment of these same rabbis was set aside because of their wish to bring joy to the bride.

Placing the bride at the center of the nuptial event, and understanding that she needed encouragement and joy at this critical juncture in her life, indicates the attention given to the feelings and sensitivities of women.

The wedding celebration is a happy yet difficult hour for women for two reasons. First, it is the woman who leaves her home and her former life for her husband's home. New physical surroundings and social status indicate significant changes. Second, women generally did not participate freely in social life in the company of men. Hence the wedding was a unique event for them. The Sages appear to have understood women's feelings, taking pains to allay the bride's sense of isolation and to make her happy, even at the price of seeming to break down the barriers between the sexes.[5]

The stories about the dances show how the Sages empathized with women and how far they departed from their customary behavior to comfort and to encourage them. The anonymous editor shows the deepest sensitivity to the bride's emotional world by the manner in which he organizes the collection.

Our Talmudic reference begins by quoting a beraita headed "How we dance before the bride," and its content is a dispute between Beth Hillel and Beth Shammai. The difference of opinion begins with a question as to the nature of the song sung to the bride at the wedding celebration, and specifically, whether to say as does Beth Hillel, "Beautiful and graceful bride!" Beth Shammai said to Beth Hillel: "If she was lame or blind, does one say of her: 'Beautiful and graceful bride?' Whereas the Torah said 'Keep the far from a false matter.'" Beth Hillel said to Beth Shammai: "According to your words, if one has made a bad purchase in the market should one praise it in his eyes or depreciate it? Surely one should praise it in his eyes. Therefore the Sages said: 'Always should the disposition of man be pleasant with people.'"

The argument appears to have been over the question of keeping from falsehood as regards a bride on her wedding day. She was considered an example of a class, since one could not accept literally the

---

[5]Although in Shitah le-Ran, "*All this* is to endear her to her husband."

contention of Beth Shammai that "a fair and virtuous bride" was a lie as regards one lame or blind.[6]

However, the main issue in this passage in the Babylonian Talmud is not about a dispute between Beth Hillel and Beth Shammai as to the meaning of falsehood, but rather about the attitude to the bride at her wedding. Hence following the beraita there is a list of testimonies regarding songs sung to brides in Eretz Israel, and regarding other songs of praise and dances performed before them. At the end comes Rabbi Jonathan's statement: "It is allowed to look intently at the face of the bride all the seven [days] in order to make her beloved to her husband," and at the very end the contrary declaration: "But the law is not according to him."

I will review the evidence regarding individual songs and dances in an attempt to find indications of the way the Sages related to women. I will then point out the connection and order linking different passages, and thereby go on to consider the editor's purpose.

The first group of testimonies consists of songs sung at marriage and other ceremonies. The second consists of reports of dances performed before brides at marriage celebrations. I will deal with each group separately, giving the English translation beside the original Aramaic.

Throughout the book, the text under discussion is presented in the original. Where various manuscripts and printed versions differ, variant versions are given in English translation. The symbols for each manuscript are as indicated in the bibliography.

A. Songs

Song 1

When R. Dimi came he said	כי אתא רב דימי אמר
Thus they sing before the bride in the West	הכי משרו קמי כלתא במערבא
No powder and no paint and no waving [of the hair]	לא כחל ולא שרק ולא פרכוס
And still a graceful gazelle.	ויעלת חן

Song 2

When the Rabbis ordained R. Zeira	כי סמכו רבנן לרבי זירא
They sang before him thus:	שרו ליה הכי
No powder and no paint and no waving [of the hair]	לא כחל ולא שרק ולא פרכוס
And still a graceful gazelle.	ויעלת חן

---

[6]The Gemara understood the dispute in the beraita as a dispute on keeping far from falsehood. This beraita is cited in similar contexts in Tractate Kallah Rabbati chap.9 and in Tractate Derech Eretz Rabbati chap. 6.

Song 3

When the Rabbis ordained R. Ammi and R. Assi	כי סמכו רבנן לרבי אמי ולרבי אסי
They sang before them thus:	שרו ליה הכי
Such as these, such as these ordain unto us [but] do not ordain unto us,	כל מן דין וכל מן דין סמכו לנא ולא תסמכו לנא
of the perverters or babblers.	לא מן הסמרסין ולא מן הסמרטין
And some say: of the half-scholars or one-third scholars.	ואמרי לה לא מן החמסין ולא מן טרמסין

Song 4

When R. Abbahu came From the Academy to the court of the Emperor	אבהו כי הוה אתי ממתיבתא לבי קיסר
Hand-maids from the imperial house went out toward him	נפקן אמהתא דבי קיסר לאפיה ומשרין ליה הכי
And sang before him thus:	רבא דעמיה
Prince of his people,	ומדברנא דאומתיה
Leader of his nation,	בוצינא* דנהורא
Shining light,	בריך מתיך לשלם
Blessed be thy coming in peace.	

---

*S Denura—of fire

Here are four songs in honor of different people in Eretz Israel, unrelated to our heading "How we dance before the bride." Instead they relate to the Beth Hillel—Beth Shammai dispute as to what one *sings* or *says* before the bride. The beginning is a quotation from Rav Dimi, according to which "No powder and no paint and no waving of the hair and still a graceful gazelle" was sung before brides in Eretz Israel. This supports Beth Hillel, since it implies that it was the custom there to tell brides they were fair women even though without a doubt some were not so fair.

Possibly the collection of songs sung to the Sages, linked to this testimony, indicates that in practice there was a compromise of sorts between the extreme positions[7] of Beth Hillel and Beth Shammai. Here

---

[7] Maybe the two opinions are not poles apart. The words of Beth Shammai, "The bride as she is," as understood in the Tosaphot, were taken to mean "If the bride has a defect, they will be silent and not praise her with this song, or they will praise her for some fine quality that she has." The words of Beit Hillel can be understood as praise in a general way (and not as an interpretation of the Tosaphot—the beginning is "Her praises shall be entire") which may be understood as not specifically linked to external characteristics, since "lovely" or "a graceful gazelle" may be construed in relation to deeds as well. A.A. Halevi cites in *Ha'agada Hahistorit Biographit*, p. 641, a song the Muses sung at Cadmus's wedding feast: "All that is loved is fair, and what is not fair will not be loved." Possibly this was what the Eretz Israel expression "a graceful gazelle" meant.

are songs sung to male scholars at receptions and rabbinical ordinations, in which it is evident that the honorees were not being described literally. It is reasonable, too, to assume that the songs were not composed for a particular person or occasion, and that they contained standard laudatory phrases said or sung on special occasions because they were suitable in a general way for those being honored.

At R. Zeira's ordination "No powder and no paint and no waving of the hair, and still a graceful gazelle" was sung. He was not literally "a graceful gazelle," but rather metaphorically so. Moreover, the puns in the songs for R. Assi and R. Ammi's ordination create the impression that these are accepted phrases.[8] The superlatives "prince of his people, leader of his nation, shining light,"[9] used at the reception for R. Abbahu, appear to be formulaic phrases, even if they are meant to honor him personally.[10] All the foregoing passages are found almost word for word in Tractate Sanhedrin 14a, which seems to have been their natural place.

---

[8]Sarmisin and Sarmitin, from the Aruch, the entry "Sarmat": these appear to come from the Greek and both mean 'rubbish.' The writer of the Aruch is virtually certain that the word was Greek, then the spoken language of Eretz Israel, where they seem also to have sung in Greek. In Aramaic, *sarmitin*, from *sirmut*, carelessly written became *sarmuti*, and this may be the origin of the Hebrew *smartut*, 'a rag'. *Tarmisin*, according to the Aruch, means 'a Roman coin', and by extension, 'one who knows only a third of a matter'. An alternative version given is that *talmisin* in Greek means 'impertinent or saucy'.

Hence there was a saying, "Ordain us not scholars from the *hamisin*, who study a fifth of the tractate, nor from the *tarmisin*, who study a third." *Hamisin* can also be interpreted from the root *hamas* as 'snatching', following the Aruch definition. Indeed in manuscript R3 the wording is *homsin* and *tirmesin*, from *tormus*, 'a cake baked without shaping it'. According to this, the song in its entirety is "Don't appoint the sages from the *sarmisim* nor the *sarmitin*, who stir up conflicts and confusion, and don't appoint sages from the greedy *hamisin* and *tormosin* who snatch things and present them without shape and beauty, like the tormos." An additional interpretation comes from the Arabic, "Not the *amisin* and not the *tormosin*"; *hamisin* in Arabic are bad-tempered people who pick fights; *tarmisin* in Arabic refers to people who chatter senselessly. Hence the interpretation means do not appoint angry people and those who have no sense.

[9]Bootzina Denahora in the Aruch mentions that in Bereshit Rabbah, chap. 75, Rashbi is called "Bootzina Da-atra" and in the Zohar in numerous instances he is called "Bootzina Kadisha." Moreover, Nahora or Nahorai is a common honorific in the Babylonian Talmud for a Tanna, an Amora, or a woman, e.g., in Shabbat 116, "R. Nehemiah was called by Rabbi Nahorai, because he enlightened the eyes of scholars in the Law."

[10]From Yoma 73b we learn that R. Abbahu was an important man and close to the Emperor, "Granted (that they could not say anything against) R. Abbahu because of the high regard that the Imperial House had for him" (Soncino). And in Hagigah 14a, it is said about someone that he raised the status of his generation "like R. Abbahu, who was close to the Emperor."

How We Dance before the Bride

The collection is relevant in Ketubot because the very song sung to R. Zeira at his ordination ceremony was, according to R. Dimi, sung to brides in Eretz Israel. It seems, too, that the editor wanted to show that the whole question of truth and falsehood is irrelevant to a wedding song of praise, as it does not describe a particular bride, but rather a category. As in ceremonies honoring scholars, one does not seek absolute truth here. Just as R. Zeira is not "a graceful gazelle" in any literal sense, and nonetheless was honored by this song, so one can in all honesty sing it to a bride who is not the fairest of the fair without transgressing the commandment to keep far from falsehood.

B. Dances

Dance 1

They tell of R. Judah bar Ila'I	אמרו עליו על רבי יהודה בר אילעאי
That he used to take a myrtle twig	שהיה נוטל בד של הדס
And dance before the bride	ומרקד לפני הכלה
And say: beautiful and graceful bride.	ואמר כלה נאה וחסודה

Dance 2

Samuel the son of R. Isaac	רב שמואל בר רב יצחק
Danced with three [twigs].	מרקד אתלת
R. Zeira said:	ואמר ר' זירא
The old man is putting us to shame.	קא מכסיף לן סבא*
When he died	כי נח נפשיה
A pillar of fire came	אפסיק עמודא דנורא
Between him and the whole of the rest of the world	בין דידיה לכולי עלמא
And there is a tradition that a pillar of fire has made such a separation either for one in a generation or for two in a generation only.	וגמירי דלא אפסיק עמודא דנורא אלא אי לחד בדרא** אי לתרי בדרא
R. Zeira said:	ואמר ר' זירא
His twig benefited the old man.	אהנייה ליה שוטיתיה לסבא***
And some say: His folly benefited the old man.	ואמרי לה שטותיה לסבא****
And some say: His habit benefited the old man.	ואמרי לה שיטתיה לסבא*****

Dance 3
R. Aha
Took her on his shoulder and danced [with her]
The Rabbis said to him: May we [also] do that?

He said to them: If they are on you like a beam
[then it is] all right
And if not [you may] not

רב אחא
מרכיב לה אכתפיה ומרקד

אמרו ליה רבנן
אנן מהו למיעבד הכי

אמר להו
אי דמיין עלייכו ככשורא לחיי
ואי לא לא

---

*   Between the lines in RD: Said (R. Zeira): Leave him. He knows what he is doing. HP carries the same addition.
**   RB, RD: the sentence is missing.
***   RA: shtutey, 'his foolishness'.
****   M: shitatah, 'his method'; HP: shatitutey, 'his foolishness'; RA: shititey, 'his method'; RB: shitatey, 'his method'; RC: shatyuta (?).
***** RA: shutitey, 'his branch' (?); RB: shtutey, 'his foolishness'; RC, HP: the whole sentence is missing.

These passages showing that Sages of Israel danced with or before different brides are the central subject of our discussion.

The testimonies indicate how the editor of the Babylonian Talmud arranged and edited various stories from Eretz Israel with a view to showing that physical expressions of feeling that generally appear undignified may be quite proper and even desirable when their purpose is to entertain the bride at her wedding.

This collection is directly connected with the title cited at the beginning of the discussion: "How we dance before the bride." However the first story is also linked to the collection of songs before it, whose theme is what is *said* to the bride and not how one dances before her, because it completes the moral lesson. This first story tells about R. Judah bar Ila'i, who danced before the bride singing "beautiful and graceful bride," the very words disputed by Beth Hillel and Beth Shammai.

We return now to the accounts of dancing. According to the first story, the Rabbi "used to take a myrtle twig and dance before the bride." Comparing this story with two parallel texts suggests that in the original version R. Judah bar Ila'i did not dance at all. In neither of the two parallel texts is there any mention of dancing but rather of standing before brides and paying attention to them.

The first source, Avot d'Rabbi Nathan, chap. 4, Halakhah 2, states: "They tell of R. Judah b. Ila'i that he used to sit with his disciples studying and when a bride passed he took time from his studies and looked upon her (*mashnin bah*) until she was out of sight. They again tell about R. Judah b. Ila'i that he was sitting with his disciples and studying

How We Dance before the Bride

when a bride passed by. 'What is that?' he asked and they answered, 'A bride who passed by.' He said, 'My sons, stand up and pay heed to the bride,' since it is written that the Holy One, Blessed Be He did so, as it is written, 'And the rib made he a woman.' He paid attention to the bride and how much more should I?"

The second source, in Midrash Hagadol, relates "A story of R. Judah bar Ila'i who was sitting with his disciples and studying when a bride passed by. He took a myrtle branch in his hand and waved it (*mesha'anen bo*) until the bride was out of sight. They again tell of R. Judah bar Ila'i that he was sitting studying with his disciples when a bride passed by. 'My sons,' he said to them, 'stand up and pay heed to the bride, since the Holy One Blessed be He did so, and if He did so, how much more are we obliged to.'" (This is followed by the baraita "How we dance before the bride.")

Possibly the slightly different verbs used in the two sources to describe what R. Judah did, "*mashnin*" and "*meshaanen*," are in fact equivalents. In any case, R. Judah bar Ila'i did not continue studying, although exactly what he did when the bride passed is not clear.

In Avot d'Rabbi Nathan the myrtle branch is not mentioned. Perhaps R. Judah's action may be interpreted in accordance with the Aruch, which in the entry "*shaan*" (שען) says "clapping the hands." This is in keeping with the Yerushalmi translation of Isaiah 57:21, where מחאו כף is rendered into Aramaic as *yeshaanun anfehun* (their branches), which fits in well with the previous sentence. According to this interpretation R. Judah bar Ila'i interrupted his studying and displayed interest in the bride passing by, but did not dance at all. The word '*meshaanen*' from Midrash Hagadol is also explained by the Aruch as 'twirled' (the myrtle branch in his hands). Neither is this interpretation linked specifically with dancing.

The Jerusalem Talmud (Hagigah chap. 1, Halakha 7) relates how when R. Judah bar Ila'i saw a bridal and a funeral procession contesting the right of way, he would say to his disciples, "Deeds come before study."

This appears to be the basis of the stories in Avot d'Rabbi Nathan and in the Midrash Hagadol. Hence we may assume that the first story in the collection about dancing did not relate originally to that activity, but rather to interrupting study for the sake of paying attention to a bride. Why, then, this transformation into dancing?

The answer lies in the assumption that the collection was edited so as to transmit a specific message. I think the editor's message is that certain types of physical activity, vulgar and even contemptible in other contexts, are legitimate and desirable when performed before a bride at her wedding. Dance has elements of gaiety and release as well as physical proximity of the sexes. Relating it to the sage R. Judah bar Ila'i is precisely what makes it legitimate and desirable.

A close look at the next story and a precise explanation of all the sources in which it is cited reinforces this assumption. The next story tells of Samuel bar Rav Isaac who was "dancing on three." This story is cited in three Eretz Israel sources, and in none does the protagonist actually dance. Bereshit Rabbah 59:4 states that "he took branches (the goodly trees of Eretz Israel) and walked before the bride."[11] The Jerusalem Talmud, Avodah Zarah, chap. 3, Halakhah 1 (42c) states that he "took branches and praised the bride" while Peah, chap. 1, Halakhah 1 (15b) in the Venetian edition refers to R. Samuel bar Rav Isaac doing a special step,[12] and in the Vatican manuscript version he "took branches and praised the bride."

Here, too, the original story does not appear to have related to dancing but rather to cutting branches of trees in Eretz Israel, in order to beautify and honor the wedding ceremony, and in particular the bride.[13]

The Babylonian Talmud is the only source that introduces and develops the theme of dancing. A detailed comparison of variant Eretz Israel versions of this second story to the Babylonian one shows the Babylonian editor's purpose in formulating and placing it as he did, and, by extension, the purpose behind the editing process throughout the collection.

---

[11]Some manuscripts have an addition to the first verse. After "When R. Samuel bar Isaac died" comes "He danced on three." In this case the passage should be read "On the death of R. Samuel bar Isaac (who danced before brides with three, i.e., with three branches)." However, in the first printing, in Vatican manuscripts and in the Jerusalem Talmud, "danced with three branches" does not appear. According to Albeck, these words do not appear germane to the story, but were added from the Babylonian Talmud Ketubot.

[12]Feldman in *Tsimchei Hamishnah* writes of the myrtle, "Little wonder that around a plant so abundant and important, tales and superstitions arose. People even bowed down to statues and idols that stood beside or beneath it." 'A myrtle of Asherah is forbidden' (Succah chap. 3, Mishnah 2). By contrast, 'He who sees a myrtle in his dreams, his affairs shall prosper' (Berachot 57a). In his view, our ancestors knew the myrtle so well that the letters of its name ה.ד.ס. entered the language to designate a limping walk, and by extension a dance, first of fowls (Baba Kama 71, Tosephta Moed Katan, chap. 2, Halakhah 1) and afterward for people as well (Jerusalem Talmud Peah 1,1), in the story of Samuel bar Rav Isaac (even though in the Vatican manuscript there is another word instead of *mehades*).

[13]*Shushbita* as used in the Jerusalem Talmud, Avodah Zarah, *shibshat* in Peah, or *shibshan* in Bereshit Rabbah come from the Syriac, according to Aruch. In Syriac, *shebishta* means 'a branch or twig of myrtle'. Moreover, the Hebrew שבוש is constructed on this word, since cut vine twigs, tangled and twisted, have come by extension to mean 'something confused and at cross purposes': ישרגו in Job 40:4 is translated into Aramaic as משבשין.

How We Dance before the Bride

I present the different versions side by side in order to analyze them and draw conclusions about the editorial method and purpose.

Babylonian Talmud, Ketubot 16b-17a	Jerusalem Talmud Peah Chap. 1, Halakhah 1 (15b)	Jerusalem Talmud Avodah Zarah Chap. 3, Halakhah 1 (42c)	Bereshit Rabbah 59:4
R. Samuel bar Rav Isaac danced with three [twigs].	R. Samuel bar Rav Isaac used to twirl a branch and made a special step before the bride.	When R. Samuel bar Rav Isaac died the cedars of Eretz Israel were uprooted. They said he would take a branch and praise the bride.	R. Samuel bar R. Isaac was a doer of good and merciful deeds. When he died, [he who danced with three branches,] winds went forth and uprooted all the goodly trees of Eretz Israel. Why? Because he would take their branches and walk before the bride.
R. Zera said: The old man is putting us to shame.	R. Zera saw him and hid from him and said: Look at this old man—how he shames himself!	The rabbis would ridicule him. R. Zera said to them: Leave him be. The old man does not know what he is doing.	The Sages asked: Why does he do that to bring disrepute to the Torah? Said R. Zera, Let him be. The old man knows just what he is doing.

When he died a pillar of fire came between him and all the rest of the world. And there is a tradition that a pillar of fire has made such a separation either for one in a generation or for two in a generation only.	When he died for three hours thunder and lightening shook the world. A voice proclaimed "R. Samuel bar Rav Isaac the doer of merciful deeds is dead." People came forward to perform the final act of loving-kindness. A fire went forth from heaven in the shape of a burning branch and stood between his bier and the congregation.	When he died fire came forth from heaven and intervened between his bier and the congregation. For three hours there were voices and thundering in the world. Come and see what a sprig of cedar has done for this old man.	When he died they went to pay respects. A tongue of flame came forth and appeared like a myrtle branch, and took a position between his bier and the community.
R. Zera said: His twig benefited the old man. And some say: His habit benefited the old man. And some say: His folly [benefited the old man].	People said: Come and see this old man, how his branch vindicates him.	A voice called out and said: Woe that R. Samuel bar Rav Isaac has died, the doer of merciful deeds.	The people saw him and said: See how for the old man there is a twirling branch that hangs.

Differences in detail

The differences in the first section have been mentioned: the significant thing is that in none of the Eretz Israel sources is R. Samuel bar Rav Isaac said to have danced.

In section 2, the Jerusalem Talmud in Avodah Zarah and Bereshit Rabbah both state that the Sages wonder at what R. Samuel bar Rav Isaac did, and R. Zeira defends him. (In Bereshit Rabbah the reaction is extreme as the Sages say he brings contempt on the Torah.)

In the Jerusalem Talmud, Peah, as in the Babylonian Talmud, the Sages do not react and the main characters are R. Samuel bar Rav Isaac and R. Zeira. However the two sources differ: in the Jerusalem Talmud, Peah, there are two stages. In the first R. Zeira hides and in the second he responds. In so doing, he does not address R. Samuel bar Rav Isaac but rather an absent audience, perhaps the Sages. In the Babylonian Talmud, by contrast, R. Samuel bar Rav Isaac is directly addressed in the words

"The old man is putting us to shame," a more succinct description than in the other sources.

Only the Babylonian Talmud criticism focuses on causing shame to colleagues. The Eretz Israel sources mention contempt for Torah (Bereshit Rabbah) and fear (Jerusalem Talmud, Peah) but not shaming the Sages.

In Section 3, all Eretz Israel sources describe the death of R. Samuel bar Rav Isaac as a dramatic, even cosmic event. The description opens in Bereshit Rabbah thus: "Winds went forth and uprooted all the goodly trees of Eretz Israel," ending with the words "A tongue of flame came forth and appeared like a myrtle branch and took a position between his bier and the community."

In the Jerusalem Talmud, Avodah Zarah and Peah, the stories conclude with a dramatic description involving three components arranged differently in each account: fire from heaven, noises and thundering for three hours, and a voice from heaven.

In the Babylonian Talmud there is a short account with one single, forceful element: a fire that is no mere flame but a pillar of fire[14] not between him and the community, as it was in Bereshit Rabbah, but "between him and the whole world." The explanation was that R. Samuel bar Rav Isaac was not only a doer of good deeds, pursuing justice and mercy, but unique in his generation.

In Section 4, we see that in the Eretz Israel sources the moral is declared by the public to lie in the link between the miracles at R. Samuel bar Rav Isaac's death and what he did with the twirling branch. The connection, however, is not entirely clear, since each source tells another story. In Bereshit Rabbah the people said, "See how for the old man there is a twirling branch that hangs." In the Jerusalem Talmud, Avodah Zarah, "Come and see what a sprig of cedar has done for this old man." In Peah, "Come and see this old man, how his branch vindicates him." According to R. Zeira in the Babylonian Talmud, the link between what happened at R. Samuel bar Rav Isaac's death and his deeds is quite clear.

---

[14]In Moed Katan 25a the pillar of fire appears in the story of Rav Huna's death, to honor him because he preached the Law in Israel. In Ketubot 62b, a pillar of fire is said to precede R. Yannai's son-in-law when he returned home on the Sabbath eve to fulfill the commandment of marital duty. (The parallel story in the Jerusalem Talmud Bichurim does not mention either a pillar of fire or marital duty.) In Ketubot 77b the pillar of fire appears at the death of Hannina bar Pappa, who observed all the commandments of the Law and braved danger to study the Law. In Nazir 7b the pillar of fire appears to assist in the process of melting tallow. In Kiddushin 71a, the evil inclination of R. Amram emanated from him as a pillar of fire. The pillar of fire as a signal honor, then, appears four times: once for a living man and three times for the dead. In two cases it was for studying the law and in two for good deeds.

He says "his twig benefited the old man." Although the key word was not clear, and possibly this explains the different versions,[15] it is obvious that the Babylonian Talmud tries to present the moral as tersely and as clearly as possible.

The differences presented and explained make it abundantly clear that the Babylonian Talmud is an edited and shortened version of the Eretz Israel story. Moreover the editor's purpose was to present the deed done by R. Samuel bar Rav Isaac as actually dancing before the bride, showing the ridicule and contempt that it aroused and, in conclusion, the greatness of that deed.

Clearly the editor in the Babylonian Talmud has shortened some elements and enlarged others. He presents the two aspects of the dance: on one hand it appears unseemly, even shameful, but on the other hand its quality shines forth. For emphasis, minor details from the original story are omitted.

The third story in the Babylonian collection is about the Eretz Israel Amora R. Aha who danced with the bride on his shoulders. The astonished Sages demand and get an explanation. They ask, "May we [also] do it?" and he answers: "If they [the brides] are on you like a beam [then it is] all right, and if not, [you may] not."[16] This is not merely dancing before the bride, but obvious physical contact with her.

Once again, a careful examination of the details of this story in comparison with the previous ones reveals the purpose of the editor of the collection and elucidates the changes he made in the first and second stories. In the first story R. Judah bar Ila'i dances before the bride with a myrtle twig in his hand, but there is no description of the dance. In the second, R. Samuel bar Rav Isaac does a daring dance, one described as "with three."[17] The evaluation is in two parts: (1) R. Zera's astonishment, (2) the response from heaven in the form of a pillar of fire.

---

[15]In the Aruch under the entry שט there are three linguistic forms with different meanings derived from this root: (1) *shotita*, 'a myrtle branch' (the entry specifies its use as a plaything at feasts and that the word is derived from שטות 'nonsense'); "The staff that was in his hand" (Judges 6:21) is translated *shotita*, (2) *shita*, 'line', and by extension, 'a custom', (3) *shatah, shata* in Aramaic and Syriac, meaning 'stupidity, foolishness'.

[16]The Maharsha explained this as the root of a pillar on which the entire house rests. Since "made a house to stand forever" was the meaning given to "made he a woman" (Genesis 2:22), the woman is everywhere called "house," because she tends the house and is its central supporting beam. Hence a double meaning: If in your eyes the woman is a wooden beam, and also the central wooden beam of the house, then you should have no sinful feelings when you dance with her.

[17]Rashi interpreted "Three branches, discards one and gets one." The Maharsha points out difficulties here: (a) the dance resembles that of Rabbi Shimeon ben Gamliel at the Bet Hashoeva festivities, and if it was indeed so, the Talmud

In the third story R. Aha dances with the bride on his shoulders. A very bold and daring dance it is, here again with a two-part evaluation. First there is the general astonishment of the Sages, who ask if they can do likewise. Second, R. Aha himself replies with a distinction in principle between a forbidden dance and one that fulfills a commandment.

The stories appear to be arranged in ascending order of intensity, from the easy case to the extreme, and from the individual case to the normative rule. There is no deviation, however, from chronological order here.

The collection opens with the story of a dance at a distance from the bride, one that causes no astonishment and no reservations. It continues with a daring dance which receives a response, first in a moral that comes from a Sage, then, in an extraordinary way, in a sign that comes directly from heaven. The concluding story tells about a most daring dance, one that included physical contact with the bride and gave rise to serious reservations, which were resolved in principle by distinguishing between what is permitted and what is forbidden. The basic premise is that every man can decide for himself whether he is capable of rejoicing with the bride without crossing the limits of modesty.

Meiri's commentary hints at the structure of the collection by saying:

> Always should the disposition of man be pleasant with people, and whoever does more is to be praised. Even the elders did so, and the greatest of the Sages used to take the bride on their shoulders, though this was not permitted except to a man without sinful thoughts, others were not even allowed to look on.

Here Meiri links the collection of stories in the second part of the discussion with the dispute between Beth Hillel and Beth Shammai in the beraita, using it as testimony in favor of Beth Hillel.

The collection of dance stories is followed by the saying of R. Jonathan: "It is allowed to look intently at the face of the bride all the seven [days] in order to make her beloved of her husband." But the Talmud concludes: "The law is not according to him."

However, the collection, as edited and presented, appears to me to contain covert support of R. Jonathan's position, even if the law is not according to him. The stories provide clear evidence that one may deviate widely from the proper distance between the sexes to give

---

would have interpreted the same way in both cases; (b) with three, and not on three, should be explicitly stated; (c) why was R. Zeira amazed at the dance? The Maharsha explains that R. Samuel bar Isaac danced like three others who danced before the bride. Hence R. Zeira's amazement: Isn't this old man ashamed that each of us, who are children beside him, dance, but he is like three of us for energy and enthusiasm?

pleasure to the bride, and it may be assumed that whoever edited and arranged the stories believed that one might look at the bride in order to make her happy, on the principle that a man should be pleasant with people. Throughout the collection the editor transmits a message entirely different from the one put forth at the end of the collection, that the law is not according to R. Jonathan. From the editing and arrangement of the individual stories, one can infer that the standard in relating to a bride is not how close one is, but the *intention* in physical closeness. Hence the answer to the question of how to bring her happiness. Every man on the basis of his own feelings and opinion must decide how far he may go. The central idea is that to make the bride happy one can break the bounds of generally accepted behavior.

All the stories in the collection show that where brides were concerned, for a limited and specified period, the Sages permitted conduct that was quite the opposite to their behavior toward women under ordinary circumstances.

The disciples of R. Judah bar I'lai turned their attention from their studies when a bride passed by to observe the festive sight. Their teacher approved, certainly not for didactic reasons, since he told them to do so on every such occasion. He even quoted from the Torah to reinforce the instruction:

> My sons, stand up and pay heed to the bride, since it is written that the Holy One, Blessed be He, did so, and it is written, "And the rib made he a woman." He paid attention to the bride and how much more should I? (Avot d'Rabbi Nathan, chap. 4).

It is unimaginable that the Sages should have interrupted their studies whenever an attractive young girl passed by, to gaze and exclaim with wonder over her. Certainly they would not have told their disciples to do so.

This departure from their usual conduct is even more conspicuous from the stories about how the Sages behaved with or in front of brides during wedding celebrations.

One cannot possibly suppose that R. Samuel bar R. Isaac frolicked with women under ordinary circumstances. His disciples are amazed at his strange behavior at weddings. In some versions they are ashamed of him and presumably think their old Rabbi has taken leave of his senses, as they were totally unused to seeing him lighthearted and playful.

Even stranger is R. Aha, taking the bride on his shoulders and dancing with her. In the ordinary way, public physical contact between a man and a woman would have been unthinkable.

There is an interesting difference between the instructions of the Tanna Judah Bar I'lai to his disciples, and those of the Amora R. Aha to his. The former told them to do as he did with every bride. The latter, by contrast, does not tell them anything specific. When they ask for permission to do as he does, he qualifies his answer: not everyone may.

It is possible that between the times of R. Judah bar I'lai and those of R. Aha, departures from accepted behavior at weddings became more extreme. What were once innocent dances, performed at a certain distance, grew much more daring, with bold movements designed to entertain the bride. Later on dancing at weddings went even further, and included physical contact. Clearly some Amoraim must have shrunk from taking such freedom with brides, both because it was so deviant from their general conduct, and because of social concepts that had gained ground with the spread of Christianity in Eretz Israel. Signs of alarm are evident as well in what R. Zera says to R. Samuel bar R. Isaac, and in R. Aha's condition for allowing his disciples to dance with brides.

In any case, the story of the extraordinary honor accorded R. Samuel bar R. Isaac when he died, and R. Aha's permission to his disciples to do what he himself did, provided their intentions were pure, are evidence of a special behavior code as regards brides. This was quite the opposite of the prevalent code of conduct between men and women, and stems from the Sages' enthusiastic approval of bringing joy to brides on their wedding day.

3

My Wife Was Not a Virgin!
(Babylonian Talmud, Ketubot 8b-10b)

All cultural communities of the ancient East attached great importance to virginity both from the material and from the moral point of view.

Both biblical and Assyrian laws specified a sum of money that a man must pay the father in order to marry his virgin daughter. This was called *mohar* in Hebrew and "the virgin's price" in Akkadian. Any injury to the bride's maidenhead reduced her marriage value and entitled her father to compensation.

From the moral standpoint, the Torah states that a betrothed girl who lost her virginity as a result of willing intercourse with another man was condemned to death by stoning (Deuteronomy 22:23-27). The same condition prevailed under Assyrian (Eshnuna 26) and Hittite law (Hammurabi 130). Under the laws of these two societies, the man was also to be stoned for injuring his neighbor's wife. Thus the Torah states that a woman whose husband claims he found no maidenhead, if that claim is confirmed by examining the "garment," is to be stoned to death (Deuteronomy 22:13-22), as in Assyrian and Hittite law (Hammurabi 131, 132).

From the Torah justification for stoning, "because she hath wrought folly in Israel, to play the whore in her father's house...," it is clear that the Torah is talking about a woman who willingly gave up her virginity while she was betrothed. A distinction is made, then, between a woman who lost her virginity when she was still free, and one who did so when she was already betrothed. In the first case the result is a loss in her marriage opportunities and value, while in the other, the affront to morality carries a drastic penalty. According to the Torah, a woman who was not a virgin on her wedding night must have lost her virginity during the betrothal period. She is thus accused of adultery, castigated as a perverse woman, and punished by stoning.

It is abundantly clear that these ancient laws were created in a society ruled by men, where women were no more than subjects, first of their fathers and then of their husbands.

In such a society the sexual responsibility imposed on women was infinitely greater than that imposed on men. The maidenhead as a witness to the woman's sexual modesty assumed sacred status, and became a symbol of purity and of morality. In the Prophets and Writings, the word 'virgin' is used to personify the people of Israel when it is described as pure and fine: the virgin daughter of Zion (Isaiah 27:22, Lamentations 2:13). Hence the loss of her virginity could be disastrous to the good name of a woman, and even threaten her very life.

In Mishnaic times, too, Jewish society attached great importance to virginity. Stoning as a punishment for a woman who was found not to be a virgin on her wedding night is also mentioned in the Mishnah, the assumption being that she had lost her virginity when already betrothed. According to Tractate Ketubot chap. 4, Mishnah 3 the daughter of a proselyte mother who played the whore is condemned to stoning.

Nonetheless, from the Talmud it appears that death by stoning existed only in theory in Mishnaic times. The Jerusalem Talmud (Ketubot chap. 1, Halakhah 1) mentions decisions and disagreements from the time of the Tannaim as to whether a woman is forbidden to her husband on grounds of "warning and seclusion" (*safek sotah*). From the Gemara's interpretation of these Tannaitic sources, it can be understood that the sentence of stoning was never carried out.[1]

---

[1]Following is a list of the judgments, issues, and interpretations from the Jerusalem Talmud (Ketubot 1, Halakhah 1). The judgments are given as proof for the explanations of the Gemara relating to the statement of the fourth-generation Amora R. Jonah Krispa, "An adult woman is like an open barrel." According to this explanation, R. Jonah meant that an adult woman cannot be deprived of her dowry rights because she was not found to be a virgin, although the marriage may be annulled for that reason.

a. This is in line with the following statement which R. Hanina made, for R. Hanina said, "There was a case of a woman in whom tokens of virginity were not found. The case came before the rabbi. He said to her, 'Where have they gone?' She said to him, 'The steps in father's house were high, and [the hymen] fell away [through the motion required in raising the legs higher than usual].' Rabbi accepted this claim.

"That which you have stated means that she does not lose the right to collect her marriage settlement. But as to keeping the marriage going, the husband is not permitted to do so because of the possibility that she has been wayward."

b. The Mishnah (Ketubot 1, Mishnah 2) states: "A virgin, widow, divorcée, and one who has severed the levirate connection through a rite of *halisah* at the

At the end of the list in the Jerusalem Talmud, the Gemara states, "All this derives from what R. Hila says in the name of R. Eleazar, he who finds an open opening must forbid her to himself because of *safek sotah*." The Gemara, then, compares all the cases in the list to the claim "I found an open opening," a type of claim where there is a reasonable doubt as to the substance of the claim, although in the cases cited in the Jerusalem Talmud, the claim itself is not called into question. Perhaps the Gemara deliberately decided to compare all cases to one dissimilar example in order to indicate a legal decision in principle in cases that would apply where the maidenhead was absent.

In all instances in this list, there was doubt as to the time and the circumstances in which the woman lost her virginity. Hence although the fact itself was clear, the woman was placed in the category of "*safek sotah*," where the law called only for the annulment of the marriage. It becomes clear, then, that stoning as a punishment did not in fact exist in the time of the Mishnah, and had been replaced by less cruel alternatives. Nonetheless, the claim of nonvirginity persisted and could annul a marriage.

Thus in Ketubot chapter 1, Mishnah 1:

---

stage of betrothal, their marriage contract is worth 200 zuz and they are subject to the claim against their virginity."

"That which you have said applies to the matter of the marriage settlement, but as to keeping the marriage going, the husband is not permitted to do so, by reason of the possibility that she has been wayward."

c. The Mishnah (Ketubot 1, Mishnah 5) states, "He who lives with his father-in-law in Judea, without witnesses cannot lodge a complaint against the girl's virginity, because he has been alone with her."

The Gemara explains: "That which you have said applies to the matter of marriage settlement of a maneh or two hundred zuz, but as to keeping the marriage going, the husband is not permitted to do so by reason of the possibility that she has been wayward."

d. The Mishnah (Ketubot 1, Mishnah 6) contains this argument: "He who marries a woman and did not find tokens of virginity—she says, 'After you betrothed me, I was raped and your field has been flooded,' and he says, 'Not so, but it was before I betrothed you, and my purchase was a bargain made in error.'

Rabban Gamliel and Rabbi Eleazar say: 'She is believed.'

Rabbi Joshua says: 'She is not believed.'"

e. The Mishnah (Ketubot 1, Mishnah 7) contains this argument:

"She says, 'I was injured by a piece of wood,' and he says, 'Not so, but you have been lain on by a man.' Rabban Gamliel and R. Eleazar say: 'She is believed.' R. Joshua says: 'We are not bound by what she says.'"

The Gemara explains: "That which you have said applies to the matter of the marriage settlement of a maneh or two hundred zuz, but as to keeping the marriage going, the husband is not permitted to do so by reason of the possibility that she has been wayward."

> A maiden is married on the fourth day [of the week]
> And a widow on the fifth day,
> For twice in the week the courts of justice sit in the towns,
> On the second day [of the week] and on the fifth day
> So that if he [the husband] had a claim as to the virginity [of the maiden bride]
> He could go early [on the morning of the fifth day of the week] to the court of justice.

According to the Amoraic interpretation, there are two alternative interpretations of the claims against the bride's virginity. One is "I found an open opening" and the other "I had intercourse with her and found no blood."

The latter claim appears to be almost objective and verifiable, as declared in the Torah, although error is possible, as will be explained later. "I found an open opening," by contrast, is based on subjective perception and is thus impossible to prove or disprove.

Nonetheless, the Amora R. Eleazar declared that in the case of "found an open opening, the woman is forbidden to him, on grounds of warning and seclusion" (Jerusalem Talmud, Ketubot chap. 1, Halakhah 1). This indicates that not only in Mishnaic but in Amoraic times, the claim of nonvirginity had legal results that boded ill for the woman. "Found an open opening" is simply the husband's nonverifiable, subjective perception, and he may possibly have some interest in annulling the marriage. This he does with a claim that cannot be proved, one against which the woman cannot possibly defend herself.

One might expect that where the absence of the maidenhead was not proved, the woman's position would be rectified by casting doubt on the basis of the husband's claims, just as in cases where it was proved, doubt was raised as to the circumstances in which it occurred. However, R. Eleazar's words, "He who finds an open opening must forbid her to himself because of suspected betrayal," or as the Babylonian Talmud (Ketubot 8a-9a) puts it more subjectively, "He who says I have found an open opening is trusted to make her forbidden for him," do not improve the woman's situation—and do her great injustice as well.

Indeed, the Babylonian Talmud (Ketubot 8b-10b) deliberates "I have found an open opening" at length. The whole discussion expresses the discomfort that the Amoraim appear to have felt over R. Eleazar's statement, and over the even more extreme view of the Babylonian Amora Samuel, "He who says I found an open opening is trusted to

My Wife Was Not a Virgin!

cause her to lose her ketubah,"[2] and attempts to undermine the validity of these earlier rulings.

While the criticism in the Gemara focuses on "must make her forbidden for him" and "is trusted to cause her to lose her ketubah" and not on the claim of having found the opening open, the true reason may well be their doubt of the veracity of the claim itself.

The discussion ends with a group of stories that show that in reality a claim of nonvirginity had no chance in court. Julius Preuss says in *Medicine in the Bible and the Talmud*: "From the details one gets the impression that they had little regard for such legal claims, and that they took pains to block the immoral, frivolous and false charges common in the East against the morality of women."[3]

We will now examine how each part of the Talmudic discussion—the debate and the stories—deals with the rulings of R. Eleazar and Samuel. I shall try to prove that in the stories, and even more in the way they are arranged as a collection, there is an attempt to avoid applying in practice the unjust ruling that a husband is believed when he claims that his bride is not a virgin.

The exact meaning of "I found an open opening" is, according to Rashi,[4] "He who says I have found an open opening and has no claim as regards blood, as for instance, she is of the Dorkati family who do not have virginal blood, as discussed later on in the Gemara, or he has lost the cloth and does not know whether there was blood or not, but he is sure that he found an open opening."

By contrast, Hameiri[5] holds that "even if blood is found he says that since the opening was open this was not virginal blood but menstrual blood or some other trick."[6]

According to both Rashi and Hameiri, the husband makes an unproven claim that can be clarified only on the basis of what he himself says. Hameiri deals with cases in which there is a counterclaim or even evidence in the woman's favor, and despite this R. Eleazar states that the husband is to be believed. This is very serious, since the husband may be deliberately lying and there is no way of finding out. Even if he is not lying, he may not be well informed and hence may be making a false claim. The woman cannot possibly defend herself, despite the absence of

---

[2] According to Ri's explanation in Tosaphot (9a, beginning with "is trusted to deprive her of her dowry") Samuel is not more extreme than R. Eleazar. See note 8.
[3] Julius Preuss, *Biblical and Talmudic Medicine* (New York, London, 1978).
[4] Rashi on Ketubot 9a, beginning with "He who says I found an open opening."
[5] Hameiri, *Beth Habechirah* on Ketubot 9a.
[6] And Rashba, Ritba, Rosh, and the disciples of Rabbenu Yona in Shitah Mekubetzet on Ketubot 9a.

incriminating evidence, even if she has proof that corroborates her purity.

Samuel's statement "He who says I found an open opening is trusted to cause her to lose her ketubah" is even more severe, and is brought up for discussion in the Gemara by R. Judah. R. Eleazar's ruling may possibly be justified on the grounds that no reasonable husband would forbid himself his conjugal right and lose the ketubah as well if he had no reason. Rashi explains, "Although the husband's claim is unverifiable and can be examined only through him, he can be trusted to make her forbidden for him."[7] However, this does not provide an explanation for Samuel's ruling about depriving the wife of her ketubah.[8] The justification of R. Eleazar is itself highly dubious, since "can be trusted to make her forbidden for him" does not mean that he himself has power to do so. The exegete Ritba[9] concludes that "for him" means that it is the court who forbids a woman to her husband, following his claim, which means that the court has accepted the husband's claim as true.

Ritba based his interpretation on the language of the Talmudic discussion. How could R. Eleazar say so, for he also said: "The wife does not become forbidden to her husband except in the case of warning and seclusion...." The expression 'forbidden' shows that it is the court which forbids the woman to her husband. (This understanding of Ritba accords well with the words of R. Eleazar in the Jerusalem Talmud "He who found an open opening must forbid her to himself because of suspected betrayal.")

It seems that the Gemara itself had difficulty accepting what R. Eleazar said:

> R. Eleazer said: He who says, I have found an open opening is trusted to make her forbidden for him. But why? It is a double

---

[7] Ketubot 9a, beginning with "must forbid her to himself."

[8] Following Ri, as presented in Tosaphot 9a, he must deprive her of her dowry. R. Eleazar's statement also gives rise to doubt, because according to his interpretation, R. Eleazar thought the husband must both forbid his wife to himself and deprive her of her dowry. He took steps to expand the scope of the law, which would certainly be the case as regards depriving her of her dowry. However, Ri's system contradicts conclusions that arise from the issue as set forth in the Jerusalem Talmud. This has been proved through a series of judgments and arguments of the Tannaim, that in many cases where the husband makes a claim of nonvirginity, he cannot, or it is doubtful whether he can deprive his wife of her dowry. But he can, even must, forbid her to himself. Losing the dowry, then, was considered more extreme than ending the marriage. Hence it is difficult to accept the explanation that R. Eleazar "used to forbid her to enlarge the scope of the law," i.e., that he regarded the ban on continuing the marriage as more extreme than losing the dowry.

[9] Shita Mekubetzet, Ketubot 15a, beginning with "must forbid her to himself."

My Wife Was Not a Virgin!

doubt: It is a doubt [whether she had the intercourse with the other man while] under him or [while] not under him. And if you say that [she had that intercourse while] not under him [there is] the [other] doubt [whether she had that intercourse] by violence or by [her free] will!

And the Jerusalem Talmud argues:

But let us be concerned that she may have been raped.

And after this claim is refuted on the grounds that had she been raped, this would have become known. And even if we say she may have been raped, there is only one doubt regarding the prohibition of the Torah, and the prohibition is enforced.

R. Yose continues and says:

If we say she may have been raped, there are two doubts: one as to whether she had been raped or seduced, and the other as to whether she was betrothed or not betrothed when she had that intercourse, and where there are two doubts, the Torah counsels leniency.

Hence the difficulty with R. Eleazar's ruling remains.

In the Babylonian Talmud's reply to the issue of doubts, R. Eleazar's ruling is limited to two instances, the wife of a priest and the instance where her father received the betrothal for her when she was less than three years and one day old. In these cases there is only one doubt. The priest's wife is forbidden to him even if she was raped and the child who was betrothed when she was less than three years and one day old certainly lost her virginity when she was already betrothed to her husband and not before. The Gemara assumes that had this loss of virginity happened earlier, the maidenhead would have returned.

The discussion in the Babylonian Talmud continues to contest R. Eleazar's ruling even after its application has been restricted.

One point against it is that nothing is new in the ruling since the Mishnah (Kidushin chap. 3, Mishnah 10) states: "If he says to a woman I have betrothed thee and she says, Thou hast not betrothed me, her relatives are forbidden to him...." which teaches that a man is trusted to forbid a woman to himself, according to his own unverified claim. This is countered with a new point raised by R. Eleazar, that the husband is trusted even on a claim of which he himself cannot be entirely sure. Perhaps in the very rejection of this attack there is a hint of criticism of R. Eleazar who maintains that the husband's claim is accepted in cases where he cannot be sure.[10]

---

[10] Another attack on R. Eleazar, on the grounds that he presents nothing new, was carried out by Abaye who brings the first Mishnah in Ketubot: "A virgin is

Another attack is directed at the internal contradiction that appears to exist between R. Eleazar's words here and what he said elsewhere.

R. Eleazar said: "The wife does not become forbidden to her husband except in the case of warning and seclusion." According to him, it is impossible to forbid a woman to her husband on the claim of the "open opening." This argument is countered by "amending" the understanding of warning and seclusion as follows:

> The wife does not become forbidden for her husband through one witness but through two witnesses, but in the case of warning and seclusion, even through one witness, and an open opening is like two witnesses.

Perhaps in the "amendment" to R. Eleazar's words there is also a hint of criticism in the Gemara that a subjective and unverified claim can have the force of two witnesses.

The discussion in the Babylonian Talmud also contains two Amoraic attacks on the ruling of Samuel.

The first is by R. Joseph who claims that there is nothing new in what Samuel said. This is rebutted by distinguishing between the subject of the Mishnah and that of Samuel.

In the second attack it seems that R. Nachman himself cited what Samuel said he had learned from R. Simon son of Eleazar on the ketubah ruling. It expresses wonder that the claim of the open opening contradicts these statements of his.[11] This attack is controverted by quoting a saying of Raba: "The presumption is [that] no one will take the trouble of preparing a [wedding] feast and will then spoil it."[12]

---

married on the fourth day [of the week]...because the courts of law sit in the towns on the second day and on the fifth day so that if he has a claim as to virginity he could go early to the court of justice." This is assumed to relate to an open opening, which would result in forbidding his wife to himself, since it is impossible to suppose that the Sages were afraid he might cool off and not come to court if the result were to be loss of the dowry: what interest could they have in the wife's losing her dowry? This attack is refuted by maintaining that the Mishnah relates to a husband whose complaint is about blood, not about the open opening.

[11] This question might have been asked more urgently under Raban Shimeon ben Gamliel's system whereby the ketubah is according to the Torah. See in this connection Rashi and Rashba in Shitah Mekubetzet 10a, beginning with "the Sages ordained for the daughters of Israel a dowry of 200 zuz for virgins," etc.

[12] The source appears to be Kidushin 45b. Here he differs with Abaye over the explanation that the young girl whose father promised her mother to marry her to a maternal kinsman, and before they finished eating and drinking the father's kinsman came stealthily and took her, doing so without the father's approval. According to Rava, the explanation is "the presumption...." Abaye said: "The remnant of Israel shall not do iniquity, nor speak lies" (Zephaniah 3:13).

Perhaps quoting Raba is an attempt of the Gemara to give a principled response to the difficulties inherent in the rulings both of Samuel and of R. Eleazar. The answer lies in the assumption that a reasonable husband does not forego of his own free will something that he has wanted and labored for. This is the rationale for accepting the claim "I found an open opening." However, in this response which appears to be principled there is still doubt as to the truth of the husband's claim, because he may possibly not be familiar with female anatomy to the point where he can say beyond all doubt that he found "an open opening." Hence his claim is dubious even if not deliberately false. Moreover, Hameiri's interpretation indicates that the husband is believed "even if there was blood," indicating that even when the wife has evidence to controvert the charge, she is not believed.

In conclusion, from the Babylonian and Jerusalem Talmuds one can sense the discomfort of the Amoraim over the rulings of R. Eleazar and Samuel. However, they did not succeed in refuting them but rather in limiting their application, at least that of R. Eleazar, to two cases only. This was not because the husband's claim was unreliable, but rather because two doubts existed, as regards the time and the circumstances in which the wife lost her virginity, and when there are two doubts, we deal leniently with a Torah prohibition.

There is no answer to the really difficult question: Why is the husband believed absolutely when he makes a dubious subjective claim, at the expense of the wife, whether she has evidence to refute his claim or whether she remains silent, probably out of shame or helplessness?

At the end of the discussion there is a collection of stories, each of which tells of a husband who claims that his wife was not a virgin on the wedding night. I will attempt to show that the collection was edited and linked to the discussion in a way that points out a variety of practical ways to correct almost completely the injustices that could have been done to women through the rulings of R. Eleazar and Samuel. The order of the stories was determined, in my opinion, to provide answers for all possibilities and to show that even in the cases where it was most difficult for the wife to show her innocence, there is a solution to avoid doing her injustice. I will try to prove that the editor of the collection wanted to show that *no* claim of nonvirginity had a chance in the rabbinical courts.

This issue is about an actual feast, and the disagreement is between Abaye and Rava. In this issue, as in Yebamot 107a, which also cites the saying "It is a presumption that one does not trouble to prepare a banquet and then forfeit it." A right is said to be valid from its inception, so that the exercise of it is different in this case than it is in our discussion, where it is considered retroactive.

The collection contains six stories, the second one in two versions, so that one may say that there are seven stories.

All the cases except the first were heard before Israeli Tannaim. The stories are not arranged according to any external common element: they are not cases heard by one man or about one man; they are not ordered as evidence in the discussion of one particular matter, nor are they in chronological order.

The judge in the first story is *R. Nachman* and in the second *Rabban Gamaliel* (in the Munich manuscript: Rabban Gamaliel bar Rabbi, and in Rome Manuscript 3: Rabban Simon b. Gamaliel bar Rabbi, even though the son of Rabbi was Rabban Gamaliel and not Simon b. Gamaliel).

In the third story the judge was *Rabban Gamaliel bar Rabbi* (Rome Manuscript 3 has, once again, Rabban Simon b. Gamaliel bar Rabbi.)

The judge in the fourth story is again *Rabban Gamaliel bar Rabbi*, with no differences in the manuscripts.

In the fifth story the judge is *Rabban Gamaliel the Elder* and in the sixth, *Rabbi*.

According to all the versions, it is clear that the stories are not arranged chronologically. Moreover, it is plain that the stories have been edited and arranged with reference to content and style.

The first two deal with the contention "I found an open opening." In neither is there an unequivocal decision as to the claim itself. The relationship between the two stories and the reason they are ordered as they are is dealt with later on.

The next four stories deal with the claim "I had intercourse and found no blood," not mentioned at all in the previous discussion. In all four stories there is a counterclaim of the wife and a clear decision, always in the identical words "Go, be happy with thy bargain." There are two subgroups, in accordance with the wife's counterclaim.

In the third story the wife claims: *"I was a virgin."*

In the fourth story the wife claims: *"I am still a virgin."*

In the fifth story the wife claims: *"I am of the Dorkati family,"* which is in effect saying "I was a virgin."

In the sixth story the wife claims: *"I was still a virgin."* From the context, this means: *"I am still a virgin."* (Thus in Rome Manuscript 1 and in Rome 3 "I was" is erased and the equivalent of "I am" is written between the lines.)

The reaction of the Amoraim appears between the stories, and from them several things may be learned:

a. The stories do not appear to have been brought to the study house as a collection. They were collected and arranged deliberately with the reactions of the Amoraim as links between

My Wife Was Not a Virgin!

them. (Possibly the third and fourth stories were a separate collection describing two cases brought before Rabban Gamaliel bar Rabbi.)

b. From the names of some of the Amoraim whose reactions are noted, one learns that the editing took place at a very late period.

c. From the reactions placed after the third and fourth stories, and the dispute placed after the fifth one, conclusions may be drawn as to the editor's purpose, as we will see below.

We now will examine each story separately, its message and the reaction of the Amoraim to it. After that we will note how the material was arranged in order to convey a general message.

The first story, the only one in which a decision was given by an Amora (Rav Nachman) is directly connected to the Gemara's discussion, since it was Rav Nachman who cited Samuel's ruling that the Sages "trusted him so that when he said I have found an open opening, he is believed to deprive her of her ketubah."[13]

The story is as follows:

ההוא דאתא לקמיה דרב נחמן
אמר ליה פתח פתוח מצאתי
אמר ליה רב נחמן
אסבוהו כופרי מברכתא חביטא ליה

> Someone came before R. Nachman [and] said to him: I have found an open opening. R. Nachman answered: Lash him with palm-switches; harlots lie prostrate before him.

Without going into the niceties of translation, the generally accepted interpretation "Lash him with palm-switches, harlots lie prostrate before him" suffices for our purposes. It can be accepted as a statement of fact,[14] the just penalty for riotous living, without controverting the husband's claims. It can also be considered a rhetorical question:[15] Can a newly married man be reliably informed as regards "the open opening" unless he frequents whorehouses?

---

[13] Possibly the question, "If so, what have the Sages accomplished by ruling thus?" is also from R. Nachman. However, it seems better to assume it is an unattributed Gemara question related to the words of R. Nachman, who agreed that the husband was to be believed, since this clarifies the Gemara question on the story cited later.

[14] Rashi on our discussion, beginning "harlots." See also Tosaphot to 10a, the second interpretation. See also Ran's comments on Rif related to our discussion.

[15] Tosaphot to 10a beginning "harlots," the first interpretation.

According to the second interpretation, Rav Nachman's purpose may be understood as a means to force the man to reconsider his claim, and the blows as a way to find out the truth, more than a punishment.

After the story there follows a question of the Gemara: "But it is Rav Nachman who said that he is believed." From this question it is clear that the Gemara perceived the beating as a response to lack of credibility. Thus one must understand Rav Nachman's response as a statement that in principle the husband is to be believed, but he must be further examined by the lash since his expertise on the subject of his claim is in doubt, and the lash will spur him to reconsider and perhaps withdraw his claim.

This line of thought makes it possible to clarify R. Ahai's distinction, "Here [it speaks] of a young man, there [it speaks] of one who has been married before,"[16] cited later in the discussion. Rav Nachman accepted "He who says I found an open opening is to be believed..." as regards previously married men, but decreed the lash for bachelors in order to arouse second thoughts, casting doubts on the credibility of their claims.[17]

Rav Ahai's distinction can also be interpreted to mean that Rav Nachman accepted the statement "He who says I found an open opening is to be believed..." as regards previously married men, but did not accept it as regards bachelors.[18]

In the basic version of the story, without Rav Ahai's later explanation, Rav Nachman made no distinction between bachelors and previously married men. Henceforth, whether we explain the beating as a punishment or as a method of examination, we must admit that Rav Nachman's decision was an attempt to discourage men from coming to court with this particular plea, and to make them rethink their claims.

As to Rav Ahai's explanation, however we understand it, there are in Rav Nachman's decision reservations about and reduced severity in applying "He who says I found an open opening is to be believed...." After all, the credibility of a whole group, one that made up the great

---

[16] According to the epistle of Rabbi Shrira Gaon, R. Ahai was one of the "Savoraei Commentators." Benyamin Menashe Levin in *Rabanan Savuraei v; Talmudan*, p. 13, quotes Yaabetz in *Toldot Israel*, part 9, p. 220, who wrote that to differentiate between Rav Ahai and the sayings of others, his were preceded by such phrases as "Rav Ahai expounded" or "Rav Ahai interpreted." Their presence in our discussion indicates editing at a very late period.

[17] Reah, Shitah Mekubetzet on 10a, beginning with "Rav Ahai interpreted," the first interpretation is preferable.

[18] Rashba, Shitah Mekubetzet on 10a, beginning with "Rav Ahai interpreted," Reah (ibid.) second interpretation.

My Wife Was Not a Virgin! 41

majority of new husbands, i.e., the bachelors, was undermined or at least was cast into doubt.

It would appear, then, that Rav Nachman's decision indicated a way to preserve the rulings of his predecessors regarding the credibility of the husband as to "the open opening," and at the same time to reduce the possibility of acting on this claim. Since there was no way of testing the veracity of the claim, Rav Nachman found a way to test the persistence of the claimant. Whether the test was applied to all claimants, or as the later explanation suggests, only to bachelors, it certainly related to the group that formed the overwhelming majority of new husbands.

Both versions of the second story tell of a man who came before Rabban Gamaliel and claimed to have found an open opening. The Sage is said to have answered him thus:

Version 1:

ההוא דאתא לקמיה דרבן גמליאל
אמר ליה פתח פתוח מצאתי
אמר ליה שמא הטיתה
אמשול לך משל למה הדבר דומה
לאדם שהיה מהלך באישון לילה ואפלה
היטה מצאו פתוח, לא היטה מצאו סגור

> Someone who came before Rabban Gamaliel [and] said to him, I have found an "open opening." He [Rabban Gamaliel] answered him: Perhaps you moved aside. I will give you an illustration: To what is this like? To a man who was walking in the deep darkness of the night [and came to his house and found the door locked]; if he moves aside [the bolt of the door] he finds it open, if he does not move aside [the bolt of the door] he finds it locked.

Version 2:

איכא דאמרי הכי אמר ליה
שמא במזיד הטית
ועקרת לדשא ועברא
אמשול לך משל למה הדבר דומה
לאדם שהיה מהלך באישון לילה ואפלה
היטה במזיד מצאו פתוח, לא היטה במזיד מצאו נעול

> Some say [that] he answered him thus: Perhaps you moved aside willfully and you tore away the door and the bar.

> I will give you an illustration: To what is this like? To a man who was walking in the deep darkness of the night [and came to his house and found the door locked]. If he moves aside [the bolt of the door] willfully he finds it open. If he does not move aside [the bolt of the door] willfully he finds it locked.

The Rishonim dealt with the difference between Rabban Gamaliel's decision, as described in this story, and that of Rav Nachman. Ravad[19] interpreted the second story to mean those cases in which the wife claims "you moved aside" against her husband. In such a case, the wife would be believed, but Rabban Gamaliel wanted to win the husband over and make peace between him and his wife.

An old interpretation in Shitah Mekubetzet[20] explains it (apparently according to the distinction made by R. Ahai) to mean that he was married before, so they did not beat him. Neither of these interpretations, however, is in accordance with the literal sense of the story.

A better explanation is that there were, in fact, different decisions. Possibly Rabban Gamaliel's liberal decision was not known to Rav Nachman. On the other hand, he may have known of it but nonetheless decided differently, given the circumstances of the case before him, and knowing that in principle he did not contradict Rabban Gamaliel, since he too spurred the complainant to second thoughts.

Interestingly, the editor of the collection first presented the story of R. Nachman, apparently because R. Nachman took part in the debate above. Then he juxtaposed the story of Rabban Gamaliel's different decision. Rabban Gamaliel, while he did not reject the husband's plea outright, expressed his doubts about it quite openly, expounding them both directly and by means of a parable.

Rabban Gamaliel showed the husband by both these means how very likely he was to have been mistaken. He turned the husband's attention to something he might not have noticed previously, through which the truth of his claim could be tested. As Rid points out,[21] "If he answered clearly, I made no mistake, she was forbidden to him, but if he remained silent, Rabban Gamaliel perceived the doubt, and the claim was not clear, so she was permitted to him."

What we have here is a clear doubt as to the reliability of the husband, along with another way to maintain the principle of "He who says, I found an open opening, is to be believed..." while at the same time reducing the damage that such a decision might cause.

The arrangement of the foregoing material indicates the intent to show them as complementary rather than contradictory, bringing in additional means of reducing the validity of claims based on the "open opening."

---

[19]Ravad, Shitah Mekubetzet on 10, beginning with "Perhaps you went astray."
[20]Shitah Mekubetzet (ibid.).
[21]Tosaphot Rid to 10a.

The first story tells of a violent way to discourage the husband. This is a flawed measure, whose general use cannot be justified, and might well discourage those with valid claims.

The second story tells of a gentler method that teaches but does not frighten.

Placing these stories one after the other leads of necessity to the conclusion that the "open opening" can neither be proved nor denied. However, by exerting various influences on the husband it is possible to reach a certain level of clarification: perhaps these are presented as answers to cover all possibilities.

The next group of stories all deal with a claim that can be examined objectively: "I had intercourse and found no blood."

This claim does not even appear in the Gemara discussion. The only way to explain its inclusion in the collection, then, is the editor's desire to make a more widely valid point. And what is this point?

On the principle that the husband who says: "I found an open opening" is to be believed, by logical extension, the one who says "I had intercourse and found no blood" is even more credible. One assumes that such a claim would not be made without the ability to show proof. However, all four stories before us go against this type of logic: in each the wife appeals against the conclusion her husband has drawn and in all cases the decision is that the wife's claims should be heard and considered. Including them here teaches that the claims and conclusions of the husband can be called into question not only when they cannot be proved, but also when he can support them with evidence, and the wife appeals either against the claim or against the conclusions he draws from it. Here are the stories:

The first story

ההוא דאתא לקמיה דרבן גמליאל בר רבי
אמר ליה רבי בעלתי ולא מצאתי דם
אמרה לו רבי בתולה הייתי
אמר להם הביאו לי אותו סודר
הביאו לו סודר ושראו במים וכבסו
ומצאו עליו כמה טיפי דמים
אמר לו לך זכה במקחך

> Some one came before Rabban Gamaliel the son of Rabbi [and] said to him, "My master, I have had intercourse [with my newly wedded wife] and I have not found any blood." She [the wife] said to him, "My master, I was a virgin." He said to them: Bring me that cloth. They brought him the cloth. He soaked it in water and he washed it and found on it a good many drops of blood.

[Thereupon] he [Rabban Gamaliel] said to him [the husband]: Go, be happy with thy bargain.

According to this story Rabban Gamaliel the son of Rabbi carried out an additional, more thorough examination of the evidence, i.e., of the cloth. This supported the wife's claims. The Gemara also cites the reaction of Huna Mar son of Rava of Parazkia, a later Amora who studied under Rav Ashi, to the act of Rabban Gamaliel, son of Rabbi: "Shall we do likewise?" And Rav Ashi answers:

גיהוץ שלנו ככיבוס שלהם
ואי אמרת נעביד גיהוץ
מעברא ליה חומרתא

Our laundry work is like their washing. And if you say let us do laundry work, [my answer is] the smoothing stone will remove it.

Possibly this response is an attempt to see a precedent in the earlier decision of Rabban Gamaliel the son of Rabbi, and to apply his system in Babylonia, to similar problems that until the later time of Rav Ashi had not found a legal solution based on principle. From Rav Ashi's response to Huna Mar son of Rava of Parazkia one may conclude that the latter's proposal was not accepted because of different procedures for laundering garments and bedclothes, in other words, for technical reasons. It was not a rejection in principle.[22]

---

[22] Herschberg in *Hayei Tarbut be-Israel*, p. 293, writes, "The care of linens in Eretz Israel was completed when they had been washed, if the laundry was properly done, but in Babylonia, an ironing was required." "Our ironing is like their washing" (Ketubot 10b, Ta'anit 29b)."For their water was good for washing, or they had good preparations for washing, and in our washing the garment is not clean until it is ironed." The term for ironing is *homrata*, the Persian word for a stone that smooths and polishes: after the garment is cleaned by washing, it is passed through a ring to smooth it. In the language of Ishmael it is called *eldakul* and the ring is called *madkelah* (from Tshuvot Ha-geonim Harkavi 60, 249). All this shows that ironing was practiced in Babylonia, meaning that the care of the garment meant not only washing, but a subsequent smoothing process with the *homrata*. Afterward, it would be impossible to find a spot of blood, while in Israel the test for the spot was made by soaking the garment in water.

"Our ironing is like their washing" may also be understood somewhat differently, by assuming that in Babylonia it was not the practice to wash garments in water but merely to iron (rub) them. Hence it would have been impossible to stop the laundering process in the middle to examine for a blood spot. However Ta'anit 9b indicates that the first understanding is more correct, since it implies that washing in Babylonia did not complete the cleaning process, which required ironing that would clean the garment the way washing did in Eretz Israel.

The second story

ההוא דאתא לקמיה דרבן גמליאל ברבי
אמר ליה רבי בעלתי ולא מצאתי דם
אמרה ליה רבי עדיין בתולה אני
אמר להן הביאו לי שתי שפחות
אחת בתולה ואחת בעולה
הביאו לו והושיבן על פי חבית של יין
בעולה ריחה נודף בתולה אין ריחה נודף
אף זו הושיבה ולא היה ריחה נודף
אמר לו לך זכה במקחך

> Someone came before Rabban Gamaliel the son of Rabbi [and] said to him, "My master, I have had intercourse [with my newly wedded wife] and I have not found any blood." She [the wife] said to him, "My master, I am still a virgin." He [then] said to them: Bring me two handmaids, one a virgin and one who had intercourse with a man. They brought to him [two such handmaids], and he placed them upon a cask of wine. [In the case of] the one who was no more a virgin its smell went through, [in the case of the virgin the smell did not go through. He [then] placed this one [the young wife] also [on a cask of wine], and its smell did not go through. He [then] said to him: Go, be happy with thy bargain.

Here, too, Rabban Gamaliel the son of Rabbi carried out a further test, and did not accept as evidence the results of the first test, which must have been in the possession of the husband. Here, however, the test was carried out on the wife herself. After this story too an editorial question and answer are introduced into the Gemara.

ונבדוק מעיקרה בגווה
גמרא הוה שמיע ליה
מעשה לא הוה חזי
וסבר דלמא לא קים ליה בגווה
דמלתא שפיר
ולאו אורח ארעא לזלזולי בבנות ישראל

> Why did he not examine the woman herself at once? He had heard a tradition, but he had not seen it done in practice, and he thought: The matter might not be certain and it would not be proper to deal lightly with daughters of Israel.

The question, therefore, is about the efficacy of the test, and possibly here too the question comes to create a precedent. Again the proposal is turned down for technical reasons: uncertainty as to how reliable the test is.

From the answer, it may be deduced that once the test was shown to be reliable it could be used in similar cases.[23]

These two stories exemplify two complementary situations as regards the claim "I had intercourse and found no blood." In the first case the woman rejects the husband's claim as false, and in the second, she rejects his conclusions about her virginity. Together they cover all the possibilities as regards this claim. After each story, an Amoraic attempt to make the decision a general precedent is introduced.

The third story

In this case too the wife rejects her husband's conclusions rather than the claim itself. She claims that it is unjust to relate the claim "I had intercourse and found no blood" to her, since for genetic reasons, a defect that runs in her family, the absence of virginal blood is irrelevant in her case. Here is the story:

ההוא דאתא לקמיה דרבן גמליאל הזקן
אמר לו: רבי בעלתי ולא מצאתי דם
אמרה לו: רבי ממשפחת דורקטי אני
שאין להן לא דם נידה ולא דם בתולים

בדק רבן גמליאל בקרובותיה ומצא כדבריה
אמר לו: לך זכה במקחך

> Someone came before Rabban Gamaliel the Elder [and] said to him, "My master, I have had intercourse [with my newly wedded wife] and I have not found any blood." She [the wife] said to him, "My master, I am of the family of Dorkati, [the women of] which have neither blood of menstruation nor blood of virginity." Rabban Gamaliel investigated among her women relatives and he found [the facts to be] in accordance with her words. He then said to him: Go, be happy with thy bargain.

According to the Mishnah (Niddah chap. 9, Mishnah 11) the Greek word *dorkati*, which means 'dry,' indicates a specific defect: "Women with

---

[23]In Yebamot 60b, the Amoraim relate to the barrel test as a method of mass examination. On the text "And they found among the inhabitants of Jabesh-gilead four hundred young virgins, that had known no man by lying with any male" (Judges 21:12), the Gemara asks "How did they know?" Rav Kahana answers, "They sat them on a barrel...."

Preuss, *Biblical and Talmudic Medicine*, p. 478, says that Greek doctors (Ionis and Euriphon) also used the barrel test. They would have a woman squat on the midwife's stool, wipe her underneath with an aromatic substance, and examine whether the smell came out of her mouth. Hippocrates also knew such methods, but some considered them unreliable. This is the only story in the collection with a Jerusalem Talmud parallel (chap. 1, end of Halakhah 1).

My Wife Was Not a Virgin! 47

maidenheads are like vines: some vines give red wine and some give black wine, some vines give much wine and some give little wine. R. Judah said: All vines give wine, and the vine that does not is *dorkati*."

This condition, then, was familiar and perhaps Rabban Gamaliel knew of it, but did not know whether the woman before him was making a truthful claim or using the phenomenon as an excuse. Rabban Gamaliel appears to have been puzzled. Unlike the previous instances, there was no point here in further physical examination. Nonetheless he found a solution and pointed out a way to investigate and corroborate the wife's claim.

Rabban Gamaliel's words "Go, be happy with thy bargain" astonished the Amoraim. From the Gemara comes R. Hanina's reaction: "Vain consolation Rabban Gamaliel offered that man." There is also the dispute between R. Jeremiah b. Abba (or as in the Munich and Rome manuscripts, R. Jeremiah, which seems more correct) and R. Jose bar Abin, who said "be punished with thy bargain," (or, as in the Munich and Rome 4 manuscripts, "You are punished"). The difference of opinion appears to have been as to what Rabban Gamaliel meant, not as to what he actually said. Otherwise it is hard to accept R. Jose b. Abin's statement, since Rabban Gamaliel also said, "Happy art thou that thou hast been privileged [to marry a woman] of the family of Dorkati."

Possibly the editor of the collection chose to present the reactions of different Amoraim, to focus attention on Rabban Gamaliel's response "Go, be happy with thy bargain," by showing how strange it is in connection with that particular story. These words, repeated at the end of each story, serve to emphasize the links between them.[24]

The fourth story

In this story the wife claims, "I was [and am still] a virgin and it was [a period of] drought." Again, the wife does not deny her husband's claim but rather the conclusion he drew from it and here too the wife's claim is verified through objective investigation that relies neither on the husband nor on his evidence. As in the wine cask test in the second story there is an actual examination of the woman herself. Here is the story:

ההוא דאתא לקמיה דרבי
אמר ליה רבי בעלתי ולא מצאתי דם

---

[24]The first three sayings in our discussion are presented, with different editing, in Nidah 64b. There, after the words of Rabbi Judah in the Mishnah, there are three beraitot: (1) a generation cut off, (2) Rabbi Hiyya: that as leaven is wholesome for dough, so blood is wholesome for a woman, (3) Rabbi Meir: that every woman who has much blood has many children. (2) and (3) are under the heading "Tanna," as they are in Nidah 8b.

אמרה ליה רבי עדיין בתולה הייתי
ושני בצורת הוה
ראה רבי שפניהם שחורים צוה עליהם והכניסום למרחץ
והאכילום והשקום והכניסום לחדר
בעל ומצא דם
אמר לו לך זכה במקחך

> Someone came to Rabbi [and] said: "My master, I have had intercourse [with my newly wedded wife] and I have not found any blood." She said, "My master, I was [and still am] a virgin, and it was [a period of] drought." Rabbi saw that their faces were black [and] he commanded concerning them, and they brought them to a bath, and gave them to eat and drink and brought them to the bridal chamber, and he had intercourse with her and found blood. He [then] said to him: Go be happy with thy bargain.

The third and fourth stories deal with special cases of the claim "I had intercourse and found no blood." In both instances the woman declares that in her case the usual test for virginity cannot apply. The stories are complementary in that the claim of not finding blood is not refuted in either. In the first case the wife declares the test of virgin blood to be irrelevant because of a permanent quality or defect of hers. In the other, the test is irrelevant because of the woman's temporary condition. Both stories taken together sum up all the cases where the absence of virgin blood cannot be used in evidence, and hence the decisions have the force of precedents for a general solution. In the case of the special quality or defect, the solution is investigation, while a temporary situation is solved by removing the disturbing factors and by reexamination.

A review of all the stories and of all the Amoraic statements between them shows clearly that the editor's arrangement is an attempt to highlight a moral lesson.

In the first group, the stories are all based on the claim "I have found an open opening." The lesson is that while theoretically the husband who makes this claim is to be believed, in practice those who did so were likely to come up against opposition and discouragement.

The second group presents cases of "I had intercourse and found no blood." Its placement after the first group appears to be deliberate. In this way the editor attempts to show that even this claim, which appears to be credible, since it would not be made if the husband did not have evidence, should be carefully examined. Thus even those whose contention is supported by proof may meet opposition and cannot be sure that their claim will be admitted.

Here there are two subgroups: in the first there are routine cases and in the second exceptional circumstances. By arranging these subgroups as he did, the editor appears to want to show that even in special circumstances in which there appears to be no way at all to help the wife, means will be found to examine her counterclaim and to refute the claims of her husband.

It seems, then, that the three collections are arranged in order of increasing seriousness as to the outcome of the case on the fate of the wife. Each contains two complementary stories which together give a general picture of the cases that the collection deals with. Taken collectively, the stories present a complete picture of the possibilities as regards the claim "My wife was not a virgin." That picture declares that while the husband is to be believed in theory, in practice there is full consideration of the wife's plea.

For the judges in the stories cited, the importance of virginity, and the punishment due to a woman who lost it after betrothal (although she was not raped), were incontrovertible facts. Enlightened liberalism can by no means be attributed to the judges; nor can they be said to have an egalitarian outlook as regards women.

At the same time, they took a firm position in favor of women who came before them in recognition of their weakness, and of their own duty as judges to protect the weak and the needy. The stories as edited and presented here indicate a consistent and methodical effort on the part of judges to reject claims of nonvirginity on grounds of principle. This tendency is evident both from the arrangement of the stories and from the style of the reprimand, explicit or implied, meted out in every case.

As for style, there is a distinction between cases based on "I found an open opening," and those claiming "I had intercourse and found no blood."

The first claim cannot be proved or disproved, and thus cannot be dealt with by the usual method of bringing in evidence. The two stories based on it show that a kind of educational process went on in the court, in which the husband was shown the weakness of his claim, for which he was reproved, in the first case harshly and in the second, more tactfully. Neither states specifically that the husband's claim was rejected, but this is clear from the way events develop.

Prominent place, however, is given to the way the judges relate to the husband. The narrator appears to do so with a view to discouraging potential "I found an open opening" claimants.

By contrast, "I had intercourse and found no blood" can be proved. Hence one might assume that there were good chances of succeeding in such a claim. Perhaps this is why all four stories based on it end with a specific statement of rejection, "Go be happy with thy bargain." This wording hints that the husband's claim was unfounded and possibly even disingenuous, and that in future he is to treat his wife as a privilege granted to him, that is to say, he has to consider her in a different light, and to try to improve their relationship.

The same directive, repeated four times, "Go, be happy with thy bargain," carries an ambivalent message as regards the treatment of women. The woman is in fact a "bargain" her husband has made, but at the same time she is his "privilege" and must be treated carefully so as not to lose her.

In conclusion, the acts of individual judges who strove to protect women against provocative or even false claims of their husbands appear to have done so to support the weaker sex, rather than to caution against further nonvirginity claims. Nonetheless, the editing and arrangement of the stories points to an editor who desires to make a protest that is based on principle.

4

Leaving Home to Study Torah
(Babylonian Talmud, Ketubot 62b-63a)

The question the Babylonian Talmud presents in Ketubot 62b- 63a is whether scholars should be permitted to leave their homes for long periods to study Torah. At first glance, the problem appears marginal, of concern to only a small group, but in fact it is one of the most central problems relating to women and married life in Jewish society.

The Talmud presents it as a conflict between the marital duty of the husband to satisfy his wife's sexual needs and his duty to study Torah, which requires long absences from home. But this approach fails to reflect the real, much more complex issue: the husband's right to be absent because of his studies involves economic, social, and psychological issues far beyond the physical problem of sexual needs.

First of all, the husband's absence requires a wife to make great sacrifices regarding her standard of living and the division of family responsibilities. Secondly, it removes her right to expect success in a career of her own, condemning her to live in her husband's shadow. If this is a division of roles, it is a completely unequal one, fixing as it does the wife's role as material and workaday, a provider of services, while the husband's is prestigious and intellectual. Thirdly, the husband's right to be away from home for long periods is based on the view that marriage is designed for the welfare, particularly the physical welfare, of the husband, not as a system of mutual physical and spiritual support for both partners.

A detailed study of the discussion as set forth in Ketubot, including the collections of stories it contains, should prove that the Sages were not concerned solely with the conflict between marital duty and studying Torah. Scrutiny of these stories and the way they are edited leads to the conclusion that the Sages were well aware of women's other hardships, particularly the spiritual ones. The editor of the collection, moreover, tried to transmit the message that permission to leave home for long periods of study depended entirely, at least morally, on the wife's feelings and wishes.

Boyarin's article on this problem as discussed in Ketubot[1] maintains that the Babylonian Sages considered marriage a sexual framework for the benefit of the man, so he would sin neither in thought nor in deed. Thus they favored early marriage, which, however, created a problem as regards Torah studies, a problem resolved by the creation of a sort of married monk, who would be away from home for long periods.

According to Boyarin, the first two stories in the collection express sharp criticism of scholars who left their homes for long periods. The first, told ironically,[2] relates to R. Rehumi, who departed from his usual custom of returning home on Yom Kippur eve. The second is about R. Judah, who would come home to perform his marital duty every week, a pillar of fire preceding him each time, showing that marital duty is as important and as sacred as the duty to study Torah. According to the author, both stories indicate that the law permitting scholars to remain away from home for long periods, while obliging them to return regularly, resolves the tension between the two conflicting obligations. The model solution, for Boyarin, lies in the story of R. Akiba, which describes metaphorically the relationship between the husband as "shepherd" and the wife as his "lamb." It follows, then, that the husband must care for, protect, and love his wife, while she is to obey and know her place as a lamb. The message in the metaphor is that all that a man needs is to find the ideal wife, one in the image of R. Akiba's obedient lamb, who, by resignation to her role, and by her joy in her husband's success, motivates him to become totally absorbed in his studies.

While I agree with this analysis of individual stories in many details, I disagree with Boyarin's approach to the collection as a whole. I agree that a late Halakhic tradition that allowed scholars to leave their homes created a serious social problem, which the collection of stories related to the discussion in Kethuboth 62b tries to solve. However, in my opinion, the solution is totally different.

In my view, only the collection in its entirety, not the isolated story of R. Akiba, is the model for the solution of this serious problem. Far from being limited to the conflict between marital duty and Torah study,

---

[1] Daniel Boyarin, "Internal Opposition in Talmudic Literature," *Presentation* 36 (1991).
[2] Yonah Frankel, *Iyunim be-olamo ha-ruhani shel Sippur ha-agadah* pp. 99-115. Here he describes the irony of the sentence "He used to visit his home every eve of Yom Kippur," and the irony of the protagonist's name, Rehumi.

the problem includes the conflict between a full physical and spiritual life with one's wife at home, as opposed to going away physically and spiritually, which, in time, leads to a sense of alienation.

The solution is to be perceived from the gradation of the stories in ascending order, from the worst to the best possible resolution of the dilemma. I shall attempt to show that both through their content and their arrangement within the collection the stories point to the true nature of the problem and its solution. The problem relates to women's position as a whole, not merely to their sexual rights: the solution is based on partnership and understanding between husband and wife, not on the model of the wife as the obedient lamb.

The discussion begins with the tradition of the Amora Rav Adda bar Ahavah in the name of Rav, according to which R. Eliezer and other scholars disagreed as to the time during which scholars might remain away from home to study Torah, without their wives' permission. This tradition states: But the Sages say, "Students may leave to study Torah for *two or three years* without permission." By contrast, the Mishnah states "The scholars leave to study Torah without permission for *thirty days*" to be the opinion of R. Eliezer alone. This tradition contradicts the opinion of Rav cited earlier (61b-62a), according to which scholars may not be away from their homes for longer than a month, even if they left with their wives' permission.

Immediately after the view of Rav Adda bar Ahavah comes that of Rava: "The Rabbis relied on Rav Adda bar Ahavah and acted in this way for themselves." This statement can be interpreted to mean either that Rava thinks positively about Rav Adda's view and says that the scholars confirmed it by acting on it, or that Rava disagrees with Rav Adda bar Ahavah's tradition, asserting that those who followed it endangered their souls. The latter view concurs with Rashi's: "It takes from them their souls, and they were punished by death."

The Talmudic editor appears to have agreed with the second interpretation, and so immediately introduced the story of Rav Rehumi, a disciple of Rava, given in detail later, which is a sharp, bitter, and ironic criticism of the scholar who left his wife and home, physically and spiritually, to study Torah. The story is the first in a series of seven, where both the first and the last tell of the Babylonian Amora Rava, while the intervening five originate from Eretz Israel in earlier periods.

Between the first story of Rava and Rav Rehumi and the second one, about R. Judah the son of R. Hiyya, is a discussion opening with the question "What is the conjugal obligation of rabbinic scholars?" There follows the answer using the words of R. Judah in the name of Samuel, "from one Sabbath eve to the next," and at the end there is an explanation of the verse from Psalms according to which "that bringeth forth its fruit in its season." This verse is explained as referring to the scholar who has sexual relations every Friday night. There are three traditions as to the Sage who gave this explanation. One places it with the same Rav Judah who replied in the name of Samuel regarding the marital duty of scholars, while others relate it to Rav Huna or Rav Nahman: all three were Amoraim of the second generation.

> What is the scholar's marital duty?
> Said Rav Judah said Samuel
> From one Sabbath eve to the next
> Bringing forth fruit in its season.
> Said Rav Judah, if Rav Huna says that, if Rav Nahman says that
> He should do his marital duty every Sabbath eve.

Possibly the editor introduced Rav Judah's explanation or that of another Amora of his generation on the marital duty of scholars, which is once a week, as a link to the story of Judah, son of R. Hiyya, who returned home from his academy every Sabbath eve. Having made this connection, he reinforced this link with the question "What is the conjugal obligation of scholars?" appropriately placed here since the Mishnah, which specifies the duties of men in various trades, does not mention scholars.

Regarding this passage as a link between two stories deliberately placed one after the other is part of a more general assumption about the intent behind the arrangement and editing of the entire collection.

Even a first reading of the collection as a whole discloses the need to determine the collator-editor's intention, because the arrangement of the stories is most difficult to explain. Later stories precede early ones. The first story is about Rav Rehumi, a disciple of Rava, an Amora of the fourth generation. The second is about Judah son of R. Hiyya—a first generation Amora. The third story is about the Tanna Rabbi who was occupied with his son's marriage. However the fourth story goes back to the Tanna R. Hananyah ben Hakinai, who studied under R. Akiba. The fifth is about R. Hama bar Bisa, an Amora of R. Hiyya's generation and the sixth about R. Akiba. The seventh returns to Rava.

Clearly stories of different periods were collected, edited, and arranged deliberately. An examination of the content, style, and parallel sources to each story will help to identify editorial intent.[3] Before examining them individually, I present the debate as a whole, first in the

---

[3] I shall not discuss the literary forms and styles of individual stories. Frankel, (ibid.) pp. 99-115 discusses the significance of the openings, emphases created by puns and contrasting parallels, stresses on places and situations (roof, Yom Kippur) and familiar motives (a woman's tear), among other matters of form and content.

Leaving Home to Study Torah

original Hebrew or Aramaic, and then in English translation. Superscripts refer to different Talmudic versions, to be given in an appendix.

Mishnah

התלמידים יוצאים לתלמוד תורה שלא ברשות שלושים יום
הפועלים שבת אחת
העונה האמורה בתורה
הטיילין בכל יום
והפועלים שתיים בשבת
והחמרים אחת בשבת
הגמלים אחת לשלושים יום
הספנים אחת לששה חדשים
דברי ר אליעזר

Students may leave for the study of Torah without permission for thirty days
the laborers for one week.
Marital duty according to Torah is
workers who work in their homes, every day
(other) workers twice a week;
ass drivers once a week;
camel drivers, once in thirty days;
sailors, once in six months
These are the words of R. Eliezer.

Gemara:

אמר רב ברונא אמר רב
הלכה כרבי אליעזר
אמר רב אדא בר אהבה אמר רב*
זו דברי ר אליעזר
אבל חכמים אומרים
התלמידים יוצאים לת"ת ב ו-ג שנים שלא ברשות
אמר רבא סמכו רבנן אדרב אדא בר אהבה
ועבדי עובדא בנפשייהו
כי הא דרב רחומי
הוה שכיח קמיה דרבא במחוזא**
הוה רגיל דהוה אתי לביתיה
כל מעלי יומא דכיפורי
יומא חד משכתיה שמעתא***
הוה מסכיא דביתהו
השתא אתי השתא אתי
לא אתא
חלש דעתה

אחית דמעתא מעינה
הוה יתיב באיגרא
אפחית איגרא מתותיה
ונח נפשיה

---

* In M, RB, RC, RD, and HP "said Rav" is missing.
** In RD the whole sentence is missing.
***M, LF, and HP add "and he did not come."

Rav Brona said in the name of Rav:
The Halakhah is in accordance with the viewpoint of Rabbi Eliezer.
R. Adda bar Ahavah said in the name of Rav:
The various regulations recorded in the Mishnah were stated in accordance with the viewpoint of Rabbi Eliezer.
But the Sages disagree with Rabbi Eliezer and say:
Married students may leave to study Torah in another town for up to two and three years without their wives' permission.
Rava said: The Rabbis relied on Rav Adda bar Ahavah
and themselves acted [in this way] for themselves.
As [happened in the case of] Rav Rehumi
[who] was in regular attendance before Rava in Mehoza.
He was accustomed to go to his house every eve of Yom Kippur.
One day his studies engrossed him.
His wife was looking out [for him, saying]:
Now he is coming, now he is coming, [but] he did not come.
She became so distressed and shed a tear from her eye.
He was sitting on a roof and the roof collapsed under him, and he died.

עונה של תלמידי חכמים אימת?
אמר רב יהודה אמר שמואל
מערב שבת לערב שבת
אשר פריו יתן בעיתו
אמר רב יהודה
ואיתימא רב הונא ואיתימא רב נחמן
זה המשמש מיטתו
מערב שבת לערב שבת
יהודה בריה רב חיא
חתניה דר ינאי הוה
אזיל ויתיב בבי רב
וכל בי שמשי הוה אתי לביתיה*
וכי הוה אתי
הוה קא חזי קמיה עמודא דנורא
יומא חד משכחתיה שמעתא**
כיון דלא חזי ההוא סימנא
אמר להו רבי ינאי כפו מטתו
שאילמלי יהודה קיים לא ביטל עונתו

Leaving Home to Study Torah

הוֵאי כשגגה שיוצא מלפני השליט
ונח נפשיה***

---

* HP adds "wait and make Kiddush at his home."
** M, RC, LF, and HP add "and he did not come."
*** M and HP add "of Judah"; RB and RD add "of Jud"; LF adds "of Rabbi Judah."

What is the conjugal obligation of rabbinic scholars?
Rav Judah said in the name of Samuel:
Every Friday night (lit., "from the eve of Shabbat to the eve of Shabbat").
"That brings forth its fruit in its season."
Rav Judah said, and some say [it was] Rav Huna, and some say [it was] Rav Nahman:
This refers to one who has sexual relations every Friday night.

Judah the son of Rabbi Hiyya, son-in-law of Rabbi Jannai
would go and sit in the Academy,
and every [Friday evening at] dusk he would come to his house.
And when he came, he [Rabbi Jannai] would see before him a pillar of fire.
One day his studies engrossed him.
Since he did not see that sign, R. Jannai said to them:
"Overturn his bed, for if Judah were alive
he would not have neglected his conjugal obligations."
It was "as an error which proceeds from the ruler,"
and he died.

רבי איעסק ליה לבריה בי רבי חייא
כי מטא למיכתב כתובה
נח נפשיה דרביתא
אמר רבי חייו פסולא איכא
יתיבו ועיינו במשפחות
רבי אתי משפטיה אביטל
ורבי חייא משמעי אחי דוד
אזיל איעסק ליה לבריה בי ר יוסי בן זימרא
פסקו ליה תרתי סרי שנין
למיזל לבי רב
אחלפוה קמיה
אמר להו
ניהוו שית שנין
אחלפוה קמיה* איכניס והדר איזיל
הוה קא מכסיף מאבוה
א'ל בני דעת קונך יש בך
מעיקרא כתיב תביאמו ותטעמו ולבסוף כתיב
ועשו לי משכן ושכנתי בתוכם
אזיל** יתיב תרי סרי שני בבי רב

עד דאתא איעקרא דביתהו
אמר רבי היכי נעביד
נגרשה יאמרו עניה זו לשוא שימרה
ניניסב איתתא אחריתי
יאמרו זו אישתו וזו זונתו
בעי עליה רחמי ואיתסיאת

---

* M, H, RB, and RD: "Again they made her pass before him."
** RB: "He had married her and then went." RC: "He married her, went."

Rabbi was occupied with [marrying off] his son into the family of Rabbi Hiyya.
When he reached the writing of the ketubah, the girl died. Rabbi said: "Is there, God forbid, a blemish?"
They sat and investigated [the genealogy of] the families.
Rabbi was descended from Shefatyah son of Avital,
And Rabbi Hiyya was descended from Shimei a brother of David.
He went [and] occupied himself with [marrying off] his son into the family of Rabbi Yose ben Zimra.
They agreed that for twelve years he should go to the Academy.
They passed her before him [and] he said to them:
"Let it be six years."
They passed her before him [again and] he said to them:
"I will marry [her] and then I will go."
He felt embarrassed in front of his father.
He said to him: "My son, you have the mind of your Maker in you."
At first it is written: "You shall bring them in and plant them." And at the end it is written: "And they shall make Me a sanctuary and I will dwell among them."
He went and sat for twelve years at the Academy.
By the time he returned, his wife had become barren.
Rabbi said: "How shall we act?"
If he divorces her they will say: "This poor woman has waited in vain." [If] he marries another woman, they will say:
"This is his wife, and this is his mistress."
He besought mercy for her, and she was cured.

רבי חנניה* בן חכינאי
הוה קאזיל לבי רב
בשלהי הלוליה דר'ש בן יוחאי
א'ל איעכב לי עד דאתי בהדך
לא איעכב ליה
אזל יתיב תרי סרי שני בבי רב
עד דאתי אישתנו שבילי דמתא
ולא ידע למיזל לביתיה
אזל יתיב אגודא דנהרא
שמע להההיא רביתא
דהוו קרו לה

Leaving Home to Study Torah

בת חכינאי, בת חכינאי
מלי קולתך ותא ניזיל
אמר ש"מ האי ביתא דידן
אזל בתרה
הוה יתיבא דביתהו
קא נהלא קמחא
דל עינה חזיתיה
סוי לבה ופרח רוחה
אמר לפניו רבש"ע ענייה זו זה שכרה
בעא רחמי עלה וחייה

---

*In M, R2, R3, R4, and HP "Rabbi Hanina."

Rabbi Hananyah ben Hakhinai was going to the Academy
at the end of R. Shimon ben Yohai's wedding.
He said to him: "Wait for me until I come with you."
He did not wait for him. He went [and] sat [for] twelve years in the Academy.
By the time he came [back], the streets of the town had changed, and he did not know how to go to his house.
He went [and] sat on the bank of the river.
He heard a girl there calling to a certain girl:
"Daughter of Hakhinai, O daughter of Hakhinai, fill up your jug and come let us go!"
He said: "Infer from this [that] this girl is ours."
He went after her.
His wife was sitting sifting flour.
She lifted up her eyes [and] looked at him, her heart recognized [him] and her spirit fled.
He said before Him: "Master of the Universe, this poor woman, is this her reward?"
He besought mercy for her and she revived.

רבי חמא בר ביסא
אזיל יתיב תרי סרי שני
בבי מדרשא
כי אתא אמר
לא איעביד כדעביד בן חכינאי
עייל יתיב במדרשא
שלח לביתיה
אתא ר' אושעיא בריה
יתיב קמיה
הוה קא משאיל ליה שמעתא
חזא דקא מתחדדי שמעתא
חלש דעתיה
אמר אי הוה הכא
הוה לי זרע כי האי*

על לביתיה
על בריה
קם קמיה
הוא סבר למשאליה שמעתא קא בעי
אמרה ליה דביתהו
מי איכא אבא דקאים מקמיה ברא**
קרי עליה רמי בר חמא
החוט המשולש לא במהרה ינתק
זה רבי אושעיא בנו של רבי חמא בר ביסא

---

*LF: "Would I not have had such seed?" HP: "I would have had such a son."
**M adds "They said to him, he is your son." LF, RB: "before his baby" ינוקא.
RC: "before his son." HP: "before a baby."

> Rabbi Hama bar Bisa went away [and] sat twelve years in the study hall.
> When he came [back] he said: "I will not do what the son of Hakhinai did."
> He went in [and] sat in the study hall, [and] sent word to his house.
> Rabbi Oshaya his son came, [and] sat down before him.
> He asked him [Rabbi Hama] about his studies, [and Rabbi Hama] saw that he knew his studies well.
> He was distressed [and] said: "If I had been here I would have had a son like this."
> He went to his house, [and] his son went in.
> He stood up before him, [for] he thought that he wanted to ask him about his studies.
> His wife said to him: "Is there a father who stands up before his son?"
> Rami bar Hama cited regarding him: "But a threefold cord is not quickly broken."
> This is R. Oshaya, the son of Rabbi Hama bar Bisa.

ר׳ע רעיא דבן כלבא שבוע הוה
חזיתיה ברתיה דהוה צניע ומעלי
אמרה ליה
אי מקדשנא לך אזלת לבי רב
אמר לה אין
איקדשא ליה בצינעא ושדרתיה
שמע אבוה אפקה מביתיה
אדרה הנאה מנכסיה
אזיל יתיב תרי סרי שנין בבי רב
כי אתא אייתי בהדי
תרי סרי אלפי תלמידי
שמעיה לההוא סבא
דקאמר לה
עד כמה קא מדברת* אלמנות חיים
אמרה ליה

Leaving Home to Study Torah

אי לדידי ציית יתיב תרי סרי שני אחריני
אמר ברשות קא עבידנא
הדר אזיל ויתיב תרי סרי שנים אחריני בבי רב
כי אתא אייתי בהדיה עשרין וארבעה אלפי תלמידי
שמעה דביתהו הות נפקא לאפיה
אמרו לה שיבבתא
שאילי מאני לבוש ואיכסאי
אמרה יודע צדיק נפש בהמתו
כי מטיא לגביה
נפלה על אפה קא מנשקא ליה לכרעיה
הוו קא מדחפיה לה שמעיה
אמר להו שבקוה שלי ושלכם שלה הוא
שמע אבוה דאתא גברא רבה למתא
אמר אזיל לגביה
אפשר דמפר נדראי
אתא לגביה
א׳ל אדעתא דגברא רבא מי נדרת
א׳ל אפילו פרק אחד ואפילו הלכה אחת
אמר ליה אנא הוא
נפל על אפיה ונשקיה על כרעיה
ויהיב ליה פלגא ממוניה
ברתיה דר׳ע עבדא ליה לבן עזאי הכי
והיינו דאמרי אינשי
רחילא בתר רחילא אזלא**
כעובדי אמה כן עובדי ברתא

---

* LF: "bear to live."
**R2: "ewe daughter of a ewe."

    R. Akiba was the shepherd of Ben Kalba Savu'a.
    His daughter saw in him that he was modest and outstanding. She said to him: "If I become betrothed to you, will you go to the Academy?" He said to her: "Yes."
    She became betrothed to him in secret, and she sent him away. Her father heard [and] banished her from his house [and] forbade her with a vow from [deriving] any benefit from his property.
    He went and sat for twelve years at the Academy.
    When he came [back], he brought twelve thousand disciples. He heard an old man saying to her: "How long will you behave like a widow during [your husband's] lifetime?"
    She replied: "If he listened to me, he would sit [there] another twelve years." He said: "I am acting with permission."
    He went back and sat twelve more years at the Academy.
    When he came back he brought with him twenty-four thousand disciples.
    His wife heard and went out to meet him.

The neighbors said to her: "Borrow something to wear and dress yourself!"
She said to them: "A righteous man knows the life of his beast."
When she reached him she fell on her face and kissed his feet.
His attendants were pushing her away but he said to them: "Leave her. What is mine and what is yours are hers."
Her father heard that a great man had come to town and he said: "I will go to him. Perhaps he will invalidate my vow."
He came to him [and Rabbi Akiva] said to him: "Would you have vowed if you had known [that he would be] a great man?"
He said to him: "Even one chapter, and even one law."
He said to him: "I am the man."
He fell on his face and kissed his feet and gave him half of his money.
Rabbi Akiva's daughter acted in this way toward Ben Azzai. And this is what people say: "A lamb follows a lamb."
Like the actions of the mother, so are the actions of the daughter.

רב יוסף בריה דרבא
שדריה אבוהי לבי רב לקמיה דרב יוסף
פסקו ליה שית שני
כי הוה תלת שני
מטא מעלי יומא דכיפורי
אמר איזיל ואיחזינהו לאנשי ביתי
שמע אבוהי שקל מנא* ונפק לאפיה
אמר ליה זונתך נזכרת
איכא דאמרי אמר ליה יונתך נזכרת
אטרוד לא מר איפסיק ולא מר איפסיק

---

*In M *mana* is missing. RB: "he took *mara*" (a handle of a hoe). LF, HP: "he took *narga*" (a spade).

Rav Yosef the son of Rava was sent by his father to the Academy [to study] before Rav Joseph. They had agreed on six years for him.
When three years had passed [and] the eve of Yom Kippur arrived, he said: "I will go and see the members of my household."
His father heard, took a weapon, and went out to meet him.
He said to him: "Have you remembered your mistress?" (Hebrew *zonah*).
Some say he said: "Have you remembered your dove?" (Hebrew *yonah*).
They quarreled, [and] neither did this Sage eat the last meal nor did that Sage eat the last meal.

Our discussion begins with the second story, about Rabbi Judah, Rabbi Jannai's son-in-law, who would return home from the academy on the Sabbath eve, at dusk (*bei shimshi* "that all await in awe," Rashi, Ketubot, 103a). When he appeared, a pillar of fire preceded him, a sign of the importance of conjugal obligation.[4] On one occasion he did not return home as duty demanded because he was absorbed in his studies. Rabbi Jannai was sure he was dead and ordered his bed to be overturned. This had the force of "an error which proceeds from the ruler," and Judah died.

This story is linked in content and style to the first, about Rav Rehumi, and associatively to the verbal formulation, in the same phrases used earlier in the discussion. Stylistically, "He used to return home every Yom Kippur eve" is similar to "every Friday evening at dusk he came home." "His studies engrossed him" appears in both stories, as does "he died."

As to content, in neither case is the wife mentioned before the husband's departure for the academy, and we do not know whether or not he did so with her consent. In both, the familiar custom is breached by the husband because he was so absorbed in his studies. Both stories end with the husband's death, though neither specifies directly that it was a punishment for failing in his conjugal obligations. In the first instance it stemmed from the insult to the wife and in the second, from the father-in-law's error. While the wife does not appear in the latter case, here, too, death was caused by one who trusted the husband absolutely, and who was therefore both injured and injuring. (The father-in-law was certain that death was the cause and not the result of neglecting marital duty. In Frankel's opinion, this hints at the vast distance between the family at home and men away at the academy.)[5]

A comparison between the story of Rabbi Judah and its parallel in the Jerusalem Talmud, Bikhurim (chap. 2, Halahkah 3, 65c) shows the editing done in the Babylonian Talmud. The differences between these two sources on the one hand, and the similarities between the first and second stories in the Babylonian Talmud on the other, indicate that the Babylonian editor deliberately arranged the Eretz Israel story of Rabbi Judah ben Rabbi Hiyya beside that of Rav Rehumi and afterward adapted it by transferring points of content and style from the first to the second.

---

[4]Frankel, (ibid.), p. 103, develops this idea.
[5]I do not accept this. It appears rather that R. Jannai had perfect confidence in his son-in-law just because he knew his greatness as a Torah scholar. Relations between the two are described in the Jerusalem Talmud, Bikkurim chap. 3, Halakhah 3, 65c, where R. Jannai calls his son-in-law "Sinai."

Babylonian Talmud	Jerusalem Talmud
Judah son of R. Hiyya and Jannai's son-in-law would go always and sit in the Academy.	Judah son of Hiyya was a student.
And every Friday evening at dusk he would come to his house.	Every Sabbath eve he came and paid respects to R. Jannai his father-in-law who would take his place and watch for him, rising before him.
When he arrived he [R. Jannai] would see before him a pillar of fire.	His disciples said, "this is not what you taught us: that a student should rise before his rabbi. He said to them, one does not remain seated before Sinai."
One day his studies engrossed him. Since he did not see that sign, R. Jannai said to them: "Overturn his bed, for if Judah were alive he would not have neglected his conjugal obligation." It was as an error which proceeds from the ruler, and he died.	One day he was late to arrive. R. Jannai said, "it cannot be that Judah my son has changed his habit. It must be that suffering entered the body of this righteous man. It appears that Judah is no longer alive."

Differences in content

1. In our story from the Babylonian Talmud there is an emphasis on home. (a) R. Judah comes to his home. (b) The pillar of light precedes him. (c) R. Jannai said: If he were alive he would not neglect his conjugal obligation. In the Jerusalem version, no mention is made of home and marital duty, merely of Judah's habit of visiting his father-in-law on the Sabbath eve.

2. In our story, we have the reason he failed to come: "His studies engrossed him," which is not mentioned in the Jerusalem Talmud.

3. In our story, there is a direct link between what happened and the death that followed, while in the Jerusalem Talmud that link remains an assumption of R. Jannai's.

4. The story cited in the Jerusalem Talmud states the need to rise before old age: hence there is an entire passage about rising, which is absent from our version.

Stylistic differences

The expression "Every Friday evening he came home" resembles "He was accustomed to go to his house every Yom Kippur eve," from the story of Rav Rehumi, which is not in the Jerusalem Talmud. Neither does the latter state that he was engrossed in his studies, which is in the Rav Rehumi story. The waiting element in both Babylonian Talmud stories is

Leaving Home to Study Torah

absent from the Jerusalem Talmud, as is the final statement "He died," given in precisely the same words in both Babylonian Talmud stories.

In view of these differences, one assumes that the original story of R. Judah son of R. Hiyya and that of Rav Rehumi contained two common elements: (a) a regular, anticipated visit and (b) a break in the habit which caused an emotional storm in the individual waiting. Since it contained these elements, the story of Judah son of R. Hiyya was included, its content and style edited to fit in with the preceding story.

The third story is actually two:

a. Rabbi was arranging his son's marriage to a daughter of R. Hiyya. She died, and it was found that such a marriage was forbidden.

b. Rabbi was arranging the marriage of his son to a daughter of R. Josi ben Zimra, and it was decided that the son should go away to study for twelve years. When the maiden was led before him, he asked to have the time reduced to six years. The idea seems not to have been accepted, so he asked to marry first and then go away to study for twelve years. Rabbi, his father, justified him, so he married the maiden and then left for twelve years. When he came back his wife could no longer conceive. Rabbi did not know what to do, because either divorcing the wife or taking a second one for his son would have injured her deeply. In the end he prayed for mercy on her, and she was cured.

Clearly, (b) is the more important story, although (a) provides the connecting link—death—to the first two stories in the collection.[6]

We do not know the source of story (a). It seems to be in its entirety a Babylonian expansion, but where is its literary kernel? Perhaps finding the names of Rabbi and of R. Hiyya in a genealogy led to the declaration that despite the noble descent of both families, such a union was forbidden.[7] Perhaps the author changed the report from the genealogies. (According to Bereshit Rabbah chap. 92, and the Jerusalem Talmud, Taanit chap. 4, Halakhah 3, it was R. Hiyya who was descended from Shephatyah son of Abital.) Possibly he worked from knowledge that R. Hiyya had a daughter, an independent and wealthy woman (Baba

---

[6] According to David Zimmerman, *Shmonah sippurei ahavah me-ha-Talmud ve-ha-Midrash* p. 32, the purpose of this story is to prepare the reader to understand the next one better.

[7] The narrator may have changed what was stated in the genealogies (making it easier to resolve the difficulty in *Yaffeh Anyaim* which states that in Bereshit Rabbah chap. 92, and Jerusalem Talmud Ta'anit chap. 4, Halakhah 2, Rabbi Hiyya is said to descend from Shefatyah son of Avital).

Metzia 44b and Jerusalem Talmud Baba Metzia, beginning of chap. 4). It was even said he had twin daughters, Pazi and Tavi (Yevamot 65b). Also mentioned are the names of his sons, Judah and Hezekiah, who were also twins. Possibly because of the story of Judah, who was the son-in-law of R. Jannai, the author wanted to expand the discussion of whom R. Hiyya's daughters married. He believed that R. Hiyya wished to marry his daughter to the son of Rabbi, who was so close to him. Since later on only one daughter of R. Hiyya is mentioned, but both his twin sons, he said that one daughter died.

Chronology may lead one to ask how Rabbi could have entered into a marriage tie with R. Hiyya, who was much younger. However, there may well be great age differences between people whose children marry. R. Josi ben Zimra, too, was much younger than Rabbi, as sayings in the name of R. Jonathan indicate (*Otzar Hashemot* 3, 831). Possibly the author of our Gemara was interpreting Yoma 78a: "I saw R. Josi ben Zimra as an old man who was a member of a yeshiva, and he was standing above this old man (Rabbi)." This indicates that R. Josi son of Zimra was standing above Rabbi. But even if our author did not interpret it in this way, and thought that R. Josi ben Zimra was much younger than Rabbi, there could have been a marriage between the two families.

Returning to our central theme, how does the second story link to that of Judah ben R. Hiyya?

In content there is both similarity and difference. Unlike the protagonists in the two previous stories, this one clearly does not want to leave his wife. Perhaps he made a mistake in marrying her, tying her to himself, and then going away to study. Even so, his father, Rabbi, is more to blame, because he legitimized the deed. Indeed, when the wife loses her ability to conceive, it is Rabbi who faces a dilemma.

The protagonist here is presented in a different light. Had it depended on him, he would not have left home at all, or at least he would have returned earlier to perform his marital duty. However, that was not the decision made for him.

The link with the previous stories is both one of similarity and one of contrast: (a) the similarity is in the subject, a man who has just married leaves his wife to suffer when he goes away to study at a rabbinical academy for a long period; (b) the difference is that all along the men in the story show awareness of the wife's sensitivities: the husband is not the one to initiate the separation and he does not forget his wife. His father, Rabbi, is also sensitive to the wife's feelings, seeking and finding a way out of the dilemma. While the story reaches a crisis, it does not end in calamity: the plea for mercy is answered, the wife recovers, and her predicament is not even blamed on her husband. (The number twelve,

Leaving Home to Study Torah

incidentally, occurs here for the first time but will be repeated from now on.)

The fourth story, about R. Hananyah son of Hakhinai, does not in the least resemble the one before it either in content or in style. His desire to leave his wife and return to his studies is emphasized as the story opens. He shows no sensitivity to her feelings or to the spiritual side of her nature, and there are no extenuating circumstances such as absorption in study or imposed duty. He does not wish to remain at home at all (which point seems redundant but accentuates his lack of feeling for his wife). According to the version in Vayikra Rabbah,[8] he takes no interest in his home and has no intention of returning there even when his surroundings give him signals that he really should.[9] Even when he does come home, he shows no consideration for his wife's feelings after she has not seen him for twelve years, and his insensitivity brings about her death.[10]

An examination of the story of Hananyah son of Hakhinai in Vayikra Rabbah shows the difference between the two versions, indicating that the Gemara is based on a narrative source edited as to style and content to adapt it to its place in the collection. A table of comparisons showing many differences follows:

Babylonian Talmud version	**Vayikra Rabbah version**
R. Hananyah b. Hakhinai was going to the Academy at the end of R. Shimon ben Yohai's wedding. He said to him: "Wait for me until I come with you." He did not wait for him. He went and sat twelve years at the Academy.	R. Hananyah b. Hakhinai and R. Simeon b. Yohai went to study Torah with R. Akiba in Bnei Brak, and stayed for 13 years. R. Simeon b. Yohai would send to find what was happening at his home, but R. Hanina did not. His wife sent word that his daughter had reached

---

[8] Bereshit Rabbah 75 (Albeck 1232); Vayikra Rabbah chap. 8, 484.

[9] According to Frankel, p. 105, the purpose of the renowned Rabbi Shimeon bar Yohai's exposition before the unknown Hananyah was to show that a great Torah scholar could still be attached to his home. Had our collection included the Midrash version, the gradation would be clear, since the story of Hananyah ben Hakhinai hints at the moral through the figure of the Rashbi. In the story of R. Hama bar Bisa the idea is further developed and has two morals. One is that the wife's feelings should be considered and she is not to be surprised, and the other (at the story's end) that it might have been better had he not left home at all.

[10] Our version states: "she lifted up her eyes [and] looked at him, her heart recognized [him] and her spirit fled." But the Aruch explains otherwise: "Her heart אסתקר." This verb might be the same as אודקר 'jumped for joy', but could also come from סקר 'see', as Rashi expounded: "Her heart saw, or her eye beheld and her spirit departed."

maturity and he should come to arrange a marriage for her. However, R. Akiba, moved by the holy spirit, told them that anyone who had a marriageable daughter should go and see her married. He rose, took permission and left. He wanted to enter his home but found that the house faced in another direction. He went to the place where the women draw water.

By the time he came back the streets of the town had changed and he did not know how to go to his house.

He went and sat on the bank of the river. He heard them calling to a certain girl: "Daughter of Hakhinai, daughter of Hakhinai, fill up your jug and let us go." He said: "Infer from this [that] this girl must be ours." He went after her.

His wife was sitting sifting flour. She lifted up her eyes and looked at him, her heart recognized him and her spirit fled. He said before him: "Master of the Universe, this poor woman, is this her reward?" He besought mercy for her and she revived.

He heard the girls say, "Daughter of Hanina, fill your pitcher and come up!" He followed her until she went into his home.

He came in after her, suddenly. His wife no sooner saw him than her soul departed.

He prayed, "Lord of the Universe, is this the poor soul's reward for the thirteen years she waited for me?" At that moment her soul reentered her body.

There are differences both in content and style between the two parallels.

As for differences in content: (a) In Vayikra Rabbah the story of R. Simeon bar Yohai's wedding and the request to R. Hananyah to wait are not mentioned. (b) Vayikra Rabbah states that in all the time R. Hanina spent at the academy, he initiated no contact with his wife: she on her part was the initiator, a detail that the Babylonian Talmud omits. (c) The greatest surprise in Vayikra Rabbah is not that the wife immediately recognized her husband whom she had not seen for so many years, but that R. Hanina came into the house so suddenly. The consternation this caused is the main point of the story, and its declared moral.

The stylistic differences are: (a) In the Babylonian Talmud the girl is called daughter of Hakhinai, and in Vayikra Rabbah, daughter of Hananyah. (b) The Babylonian Talmud states, "By the time he returned the streets of the town had changed." The style recalls the previous story, about the son of Rabbi, in which the long separation deprived his wife of the ability to bear children. In Vayikra Rabbah, "he tried to enter his home but could not find the way." (c) The Babylonian story ends, "He besought mercy for her and she revived," which is similar to "He besought mercy for her and she was cured" in the Babylonian Talmud's story of Rabbi's son. Vayikra Rabbah states simply, "Her soul reentered her body."

From the differences one infers that the nucleus of the story about R. Hananyah b. Hakhinai contained similar elements to that of the story about Rabbi's son. (a) Prolonged absence from home indirectly led to calamity: the sudden return completely surprised the wife, bringing the calamity about. (b) The return renewed feelings of closeness, which averted the disaster.

The story of R. Hananyha b. Hakhinai appears to have been included in our collection because of these elements, and subsequently emended as to content and style, to fit in with the preceding story. Thus a description that highlights the wife's unhappy condition is included, as well as the twelve years spent at the academy. The words from "When they reached the house" to "was so overcome with joy that her spirit fled" come from the immediate environment, while "he besought mercy for her" comes from the previous story.

From the connecting passage that precedes the fifth story, it appears that the fourth is merely a preface to that of R. Hama bar Bisa who applied the lesson from the case of R. Hananyah son of Hakhinai. Nonetheless, there is an associative and linguistic link between the latter and the third story, about Rabbi's son. Just as Rabbi's daughter-in-law recovered after he prayed for mercy for her, so did the wife of R. Hananyah b. Hakhinai. The common denominator is the prayer for mercy and the deliverance, a happy end.

The link between the fifth story, about R. Hama bar Bisa and the one before it is self-explanatory, as the protagonist opens by stating, "I will not do what the son of Hakhinai did." A thread of optimism is evident throughout. Here the husband's sensitive and considerate behavior prevents any calamity. The story is more complex than the others.

The family described is one where harmonious relations prevail despite the physical separation of husband and wife. He is careful not to hurt her. On Hama's return from the academy, a conversation develops between father and son, and a contact is made even though Hama does not know of the relationship. This is quite different from R. Hananyah b. Hakhinai who makes no contact with his daughter and follows her secretly: she is not even called by his name but by her grandfather's, though in Vayikra Rabbah she is called "Daughter of Hananyah," after her father. The encounter with his son leads R. Hama bar Bisa to regret that his long absence has made him remote and even superfluous. The wife, by saying "Is there a father who stands up before his son?" shows that she is not angry with her husband but concerned for his honor, values his achievements, and has raised her son to respect him and follow in his footsteps.

"But a threefold cord is not quickly broken" shows that Rami bar Hama held this distinguished family in the highest esteem. It also emphasizes, with the return of R. Hama bar Bisa, that family harmony was maintained.

What is there in this story that is not in the one before it? Here, too, the husband was separated from his wife for twelve years. Why is the end different? I postulate two major differences: first, the husband is considerate and second, the wife participates. While there is no evidence of her explicit permission, one reads between the lines and understands that she supported her husband. This is a turning point in the collection. From here on, the stories become optimistic and the moral emerges.

We appear to have here a tendentious story assembled from two origins. The first is the story of R. Hananyah b. Hakhinai and the second is Rami bar Hama's remark (Baba Batra 59a) about the strong generational links in Hama bar Bisa's family. We will return to this later, to explain the editor's intention.

The sixth story is the literary and didactic climax of the collection, and that is why it is placed where it is. R. Akiba spent twelve years at the academy, and then another twelve. According to the account in our debate, the first time his wife not only gave her consent to his departure, but instigated it.

Not content to ask, "If I become betrothed to you, will you go to the Academy?" which indicates that going away to study was the main condition the wife made for the marriage, the story adds, "She became betrothed to him in secret and she sent him away." She it was who sent him. All the other stories simply state, "He went away and stayed...." The story of the father who disinherited her and the taunts of the old man (possibly an inner voice) are all designed to augment the wife's part. She it was who instigated the plan and she it was who stands fast against all attempts to thwart it. The second time too, R. Akiba goes away again only after he hears his wife's explicit wish. It is not clear why he does not actually meet her. Perhaps it is the narrator's way to show that what really mattered was the meeting of minds, and to add further to the worth of such a wife: although she does not know that her husband returned or at least intends to return to her, she trusts him. (Her trust is certainly nourished by the fact that R. Akiba does not forget his home and visits there before he completes his studies.) Years later, the situation is reversed: R. Akiba returns a famous man while his wife is unknown and very poor. Even then, she has great confidence, to the point where she refuses to adorn herself for his coming. Indeed, by contrast with the preceding stories, there is no breach of confidence here. We are left in

Leaving Home to Study Torah

suspense until the last moment. R. Akiba behaves as his wife anticipated, declaring before all his disciples that his wife is the true heroine in the story of his life, expressing in his short, emotional pronouncement the spiritual unity between them.

This story, then, is entirely optimistic. If in the fourth story, the wife accedes silently, here she is an active instigator. The husband is not punished: he attains greatness and honor. If the preceding story ends in a minor key, mentioning the protagonist's son and his family heritage, here a major chord is sounded. R. Akiba himself wins fame, he and his wife become rich, and their daughter follows in her mother's footsteps. The Sage's long absence harmed neither love nor family harmony.

There is a parallel to the story of R. Akiba in Nedarim 50a. Here, too, a comparison of the two parallel versions elucidates the connecting links and the formulation of the story in our Talmudic discussion:

The R. Akiba story in Ketubot

R. Akiba was a shepherd of Ben Kalba Savu'a. His daughter saw [in] him that he was modest and outstanding. She said to him: "If I become betrothed to you, will you go to the Academy?" He said to her: "Yes." She became betrothed to him in secret and sent him away. Her father heard [and] banished her from his house [and] forbade her with a vow from [deriving any] benefit from his property. He went [and] sat for twelve years in the Academy.
When he came [back] he brought with him twelve thousand disciples.
He heard an old man saying to her: "For how long will you behave like a widow during [your husband's] lifetime?" She said to him: "If he would listen to me, he would sit [there] twelve more years." He said: "I am acting then with her permission." He went back and sat twelve more years in the Academy. When he came [back] he brought with him twenty-four thousand disciples. His wife heard and went out to [greet] him. The neighbors said to her: "Borrow something to wear and dress yourself!"
She said to them: "A righteous man knows the life of his beast."

The R. Akiba story in Nedarim

R. Akiba betrothed the daughter of (the son of) Kalba Savu'a.

(The son of) Kalba Savu'a heard and disinherited her. She married him and in the fall they slept in the barn. He picked the straw out of her hair and said, "I would like to give you a golden Jerusalem."

Elijah appeared to them in human form and said, "Give some straw, for my wife is in confinement and I have nothing for her to lie on." "See," R. Akiba said to his wife, "here's a man who lacks even straw."

[Subsequently] she counseled him, "Go and become a scholar." So he left and spent twelve years [studying] under R. Eliezer and R. Joshua.
At the end of this time, he returned home, and from the back of the house he heard a wicked man jeering at his wife. "Your father did well to you, firstly because he is your inferior; secondly because he abandoned you to a living widowhood all the years."

When she reached him, she fell on her face [and] she kissed his feet. His attendants were pushing her away, [but] he said to them: "Leave her. What is mine and what is yours is hers."
Her father heard that a great man had come to town, [and] he said: "I will go to him. Perhaps he will invalidate my vow." He came to him, [and Rabbi Akiba] said to him: "Would you have vowed had you known [that he would be a great man?" He said to him: "Even one chapter, and even one law." He said to him: "I am he." He fell on his face and kissed his feet, and gave him half of his money.
Rabbi Akiba's daughter acted in this way toward Ben Assai. And this is what people say: "A lamb follows a lamb."
Like the actions of the mother, so are the actions of the daughter.

She replied, "Yet were he to hear my desires, he would be absent for another twelve years."
"Seeing that she thus gave me permission," he said, "I will go back." So he went back, and was absent for another twelve years [at the end of which] he returned with twenty-four thousand disciples. Everyone flocked to welcome him, including [his wife]. But that wicked man said to her, "And where goest *thou*?" "A righteous man knoweth the life of his beast," she retorted. So she went to see him, but the disciples wished to repulse her. "Make way for her," he told them, "for my [learning] and yours are hers."

When Kalba Savu'a heard thereof, he came [before R. Akiba] and asked for the remission of his vow and he annulled it for him.

The two versions differ in content in several respects. (a) In our story, in Ketubot, there is a reason for ben Kalba Savu'a's daughter's love toward R. Akiba. "She saw that he was modest and outstanding"; in Nedarim there is none. (b) In the story in Ketubot, the conversation between R. Akiba and Kalba Savu'a's granddaughter before their wedding is described in detail, revealing the wife's initiative in his studies. In Nedarim, there is no such dialogue. (c) In the Ketubot version, Akiba leaves right after his marriage and then her father deprives her of her property; in Nedarim the father did so after the betrothal and nonetheless she went forward with the marriage. (d) In Nedarim there is a description of the beautiful relationship between R. Akiba and his wife, and of the incident that led indirectly to his departure for the academy. One infers that it was he who wanted to go away to study, while she hesitated to face a life of poverty. He reproves—or encourages—her when he says, "See this man who lacks even straw." (e) Ketubot relates simply that he studied at the academy, while Nedarim specifies that he studied at the academy of R. Eliezer and R. Joshua. (f) Our story tells of an old man who asked the wife, "For how long will you behave like a widow during your husband's lifetime?" Nedarim, by contrast, tells of a wicked man who reproved her on two counts: he is your inferior and he abandoned you to live like a widow. (g) Nedarim does not report that twelve thousand disciples came with R. Akiba on his first return. (h) In Ketubot, the story of the second return focuses on the wife: she goes out to meet him, while in Nedarim she is simply with "everyone" who does so. (i) In Ketubot, well-meaning neighbors offer help, while in Nedarim the wicked man who taunted her before does so again. (j) The actual meeting between his wife and R. Akiba is described in more detail in Ketubot: "She fell upon her face and kissed his feet." (k) The meeting of Kalba Savu'a's son and R. Akiba is detailed in Ketubot: content lacking in Nedarim explains why the vow was annulled. (l) The story of R. Akiba's daughter and the saying it illustrates are not found in Nedarim.

Given all these differences, one may assume certain details in the nucleus of the R. Akiba story: the daughter of Kalba Savu'a's son fell in love with him when he was poor, married him, angered her father, and was forced into poverty; R. Akiba began to study at a relatively advanced age; R. Akiba went far as a scholar and had many disciples; the love between him and his wife continued despite their long separation. (All these elements except for the first are found in the account of R. Akiba's early years in Avoth d'Rabbi Nathan chap. 6.)

The story of R. Akiba is placed in the Ketubot collection after that of Hama bar Bisa where, as previously stated, a thread of optimism is visible. Hama bar Bisa showed consideration for his wife despite their long separation, so she did not suffer mental anguish like R. Rehumi's wife, or physical harm like the wife of Rabbi's son. The spiritual relationship between husband and wife that is merely suggested in the story of Hama bar Bisa is clearly presented in that of R. Akiba. There are similarities in content too: Hama bar Bisa sends to inform his wife that he is coming; while she does not go out to meet him, instead she sends her son, thus taking part indirectly in the return scene. R. Akiba does not inform his wife of his coming, but she participates unobserved in the first arrival scene. Even before he finds out that the scholarly youth is his son, Hama bar Bisa regrets his long absence; Kalba Savu'a's son regrets his vow even before he learns that the great rabbi who has come to town is his son-in-law. Hama bar Bisa's story ends with the son who follows in his footsteps, the family serving as the subject of a wise saying; R. Akiba's story concludes with the daughter who walks in the ways of her mother, relating the family to another popular adage.

From the differences between the R. Akiba story in the Ketubot and Nedarim versions, and from a comparison of the former with its predecessor in the collection, one may conclude that the nucleus of the R. Akiba story had elements in common with the one existing or composed about Hama bar Bisa. In both the long separation ended without a crisis, and conjugal life bore blessed fruit. Their juxtaposition appears to be the result of their common basis, with changes in content made as an adaptation to the place in the collection. The wife's role is emphasized and she becomes the protagonist, thus introducing the motifs of reward and continuity.

Examining the points of resemblance within the story dyads—the first and second, third and fourth, fifth and sixth—and the contrasts between the second, fourth, and sixth stories as they appear in our collection and their parallels in other sources, a conclusion emerges: the stories were edited and arranged to teach a moral and social lesson. In my opinion, that lesson, the purpose of the collection, is to show that in no case is the study of Torah to be preferred above family life, if it renders the wife miserable. Leaving home to study Torah is justified only if the wife is a full partner in the decision and if the spiritual link between husband and wife is maintained. In other words, the negative aspect of leaving home is not physical but spiritual separation, where complete immersion in the Torah world severs connections with home and family.

On this principle, the stories were arranged in dyads, each presenting a different type of relationship. Each dyad has its own internal order and its own moral. The composite lesson is that the wife's consent is a necessary condition for leaving home to study Torah.

The seventh story is included, it would seem, to highlight the conflict between the will to study and unwillingness to leave one's wife.[11] One possible explanation is that Rava was angry with his son because he did not come home for three years, but it can also be argued that he was angry because his son came home before he finished his studies.[12] In either case the extreme language "Have you remembered your mistress?" or "Have you remembered your dove?"[13] (words with similar spelling and sound in Hebrew) and the exacerbated quarrel "neither father nor son ate the last meal before the fast" shows how very serious the conflict was.

Let us now examine the links within each of the dyads, and the links that connect them with each other.

In the first dyad (the stories of R. Rehumi and R. Judah son of Hiyya) the husband prefers his Torah studies to his obligation to his wife, and

---

[11]One cannot determine whether this story is true or fictitious. There are elements on which a true story could have been built: R. Joseph son of Rava is known to have studied with R. Joseph, and his wife is mentioned shortly afterward, on 65a.

[12]In the Jerusalem Talmud (Pesachim chap. 3, Halakhah 7 and Hagigah chap. 1, Halakhah 7) there is a story about R. Abbahu who sent his son R. Hanina to study Torah, and was angry with him because he stopped studying to occupy himself with charitable works.

[13]Weiss, *A Study of the Talmud* p. 228, cites this as an example of cases in which the second version (in our case, זוגתך 'your spouse') was brought in so as not to use any expression that hints at censure against Talmudic Sages.

Leaving Home to Study Torah

for this he suffers death. The first story tells of an almost complete separation between husband and wife: "He was in regular attendance before Rava in Mehoza."[14] The second, on the other hand, tells of a close and loving relationship where there was no neglect of marital duty: the husband would come home in the twilight of every Sabbath eve. In the first the husband is punished for the sorrow he caused his wife: "She shed a tear from her eye, he was sitting on a roof, and the roof collapsed under him and he died."[15] In the second instance, death came from "an error which proceeds from the ruler." In both cases, however, there was just one omission, just one fatal forgetting to go home because "his studies engrossed him."

The moral here is that whether a man is always far from his home or whether he is devoted and faithful to it, to forget one's domestic obligations completely and betray one's wife spiritually even once is a very severe offense and ends in calamity.

In the second dyad (the stories of the son of Rabbi and of Hananyah son of Hakhinai) the husband is away from his wife for twelve years. The separation brings crisis and catastrophe, but when the husband returns to his wife emotionally, he averts the evil decree.

In the first instance the husband would prefer to live with his wife rather than go away to study Torah, and he tries to reduce the designated period or to delay his departure. In the second, however, the husband is captured in the fascination of Torah study and is not even prepared to delay his departure briefly. In both cases, calamity overtakes their wives.

The moral here, therefore, is that separation from home, whether forced or desired, is negative and brings disaster. (One may assume that the protagonist of the first story, too, was absent both physically and spiritually from his wife while he was away at the academy.) Nonetheless, the return home, however belated, shows sensitivity and understanding toward the wife's feelings, and makes atonement and reparation.

In the third dyad (about Hama b. Bisa and R. Akiba) the husband is far away from his wife but they are not severed spiritually. Hence there is no calamity and the return is accomplished without crisis.

In the first story the wife's wishes are not explicitly mentioned, but one may infer that she accepts her husband's twelve-year absence, and raises her son to follow in his father's footsteps. She it is who plans the surprise and the meeting. The husband on his part has misgivings about having been away so long. In the second story, two twelve-year

---

[14] See Frankel, ibid. p. 101.
[15] See Frankel, ibid.

separations follow one another, clearly according to the wishes and initiative of the wife. There is clear evidence of inner conflict on the part of the husband on the first return, indicated by his words, "I am acting with permission."

The moral of both stories is that physical separation by consent, that does not cause spiritual estrangement, is not evil, and when undertaken for the sake of Torah study is a positive act that brings a reward.

Under no circumstances is one to view the purpose of these stories as the presentation of the ideal wife as a submissive, obedient lamb. On the contrary, the stories in Ketubot show that the wives of Hama bar Bisa and of R. Akiba were active women who initiated and motivated, the first her son and the second her husband, to take the road they had chosen for them.

The dyads themselves are arranged according to the morals to be drawn from them, in ascending order, beginning with the worst case: a complete severance, even if it happened only once, between husband and wife. Next comes a disorder that can be corrected: physical and spiritual separation that ends with a return to an understanding and sensitive relationship. The collection concludes with the good and the positive: spiritual closeness and a common purpose that continues over time despite the physical distance between the marriage partners.

5

Women and Wine
(Babylonian Talmud Ketubot 64b-65a)

Drinking wine is mentioned hundreds of times in Talmudic literature, which shows how widespread it was, particularly at family celebrations and festive meals, among the Jewish people. There is even a beraita that states, "Kiddush is not made unless there is wine, and a blessing is not made unless there is wine" (Pesachim 107a).

Apart from its use at festive meals, the Sages had an ambivalent attitude to drinking wine. On the one hand they realized its value and recommended it. The Gemara in Berachot (35b) states, "Wine has two virtues: it nourishes and brings joy," and the one in Baba Batra (58b) recommends wine as a medicine in the name of the elders of Judah who said, "First among the medicines am I, Wine. Where there is no wine, people seek drug potions." Rashi explains that drugs are needed as medicines because where there is no wine, there is illness. Wine is also recommended by Rav Huna son of Rav Joshua in Baba Batra (12b) as opening the heart: "In one used to wine, even if his heart is as closed as a virgin is, wine opens it."

On the other hand, the Sages were aware of the dangers of heavy drinking. Rav Judah told a certain matron that he did not taste wine at Pesach except for Kiddush, Havdalah, and the Four Cups, but his head ached until Shavuot (Nedarim 49b). The Sages warned against drinking too much, and against drinking at work: "We have learned that a quarter of a measure of Italian wine produces intoxication, and we have learned that one who is intoxicated should not teach" (Eruvin 64b). For those who became drunk, they recommended a good long sleep and a walk to sober up: "Sleep arouses from heavy drinking" (Baba Batra 10a), and "We have learned that walking wears out wine" (Eruvin 64b).

In the explanations of the Amoraim R. Kahana and Rava, in Sanhedrin (70a), this ambivalence is highlighted by a play on the second syllable of the Hebrew word *tirosh*, a synonym for 'wine', which can be read either as 'becoming the head', ראש, or as 'becoming poor', רש. Rav Kahana confronts these two possibilities: "If he is fortunate he becomes the head and if he is not it impoverishes him." Rava declares: "If he gets the good effects of wine he becomes happy, if he does not get them, he becomes miserable."

In principle, moderate wine drinking is thought good, as shown in the saying of Rav Hanan: "Wine was not created except to console mourners and to give the wicked their just reward, as it is said, 'Give drink to those who are lost and wine to those of heavy heart'" (Sanhedrin 70b). Here, too, there is a play on words: depending on whether the first letter is read *sin* or *shin*, the word שכר means either 'reward' or 'strong drink'. Going without wine was, according to R. Joshua, a decree that most of the congregation could not abide by (Baba Batra 60b).

The Sages usually related to wine drinking at the level of the individual's health, feelings, and behavior. Hence the different attitudes to the different genders is of and in itself an example of inequality.

The Sages knew that drinking too much wine could make a person lose self-control and a sense of judgment. Freedom of choice, then, clearly expressed the extent of trust in the individual's maturity and independence. An adult is entitled to decide the limits of his self-control, so that the law, too, has limits in which it can intervene to "defend" him from himself.

Against this background one discovers in the laws and the open declarations of the Mishnah and Talmud Sages a clear distinction between men and women. Men are advised and directed, but no legislation forbids or limits drinking, while toward women there is a quite different, openly declared attitude.

Following the basic concept that drinking wine destroys a woman's control in the sexual area specifically, one hears declarations like "He who sees before him a suspected adulteress (sotah) will keep away from wine" (Sotah 2a). Similarly R. Eleazar, "Wine is not awarded to women in court judgments" (Ketubot 64a).

A similar attitude prevailed in ancient Rome, according to A.A. Halevi's *Talmudic Laws and Legends in the Light of Greek and Latin Sources* (p. 251). Romulus, the first Roman king, allowed husbands and relatives to put to death a woman who drank wine, and even later, husbands and fathers could forbid their wives and daughters to drink wine. According to Halevi, in certain Greek cities too, women were forbidden to drink wine. Such prohibitions clearly resulted from an egocentric male outlook that perceived women as weak, childish, irresponsible sexual creatures,

Women and Wine

to be controlled and protected from their surroundings and from themselves.

This patronizing attitude permeates the external, declarative layer of Talmudic literature. However, the discussion in the Babylonian Talmud (Ketubot 64b-65a) contains a collection of stories about widows who applied to the courts for a wine allowance. Careful study of the discussion and of the concluding collection of stories, however, shows a wide gap between the overt declarations and the concepts that emerge in each one of the stories, something hinted at by the arrangement of the collection as a whole.

Looking carefully at the discussion in the Babylonian Talmud in its entirety, we will compare the negotiation there to that in the Jerusalem Talmud, and in the story section we will examine the different viewpoints, both expressed and implied.

In Ketubot chap. 5, Mishnah 8, a list of food, clothing, and household goods specifies what one who provides for his wife through a third party must give her:

המשרה את אשתו על ידי שליש
לא יפחות לה משני קבין חטין
או מארבעה קבין שעורין
אמר רבי יוסי לא פסק לה
שעורין אלא ר' ישמעאל
שהיה סמוך לאדום
ונותן לה חצי קב קטנית וחצי לוג שמן
וקב גרוגרת או מנה דבילה
ואם אין לו, פוסק לעומתן פירות ממקום אחר
ונותן לה מטה מפץ ומחצלת
ונותן לה כפה לראשה וחגור למותניה
ומנעלים ממועד למועד
וכלים של חמישים זוז משנה לשנה
ואין נותנים לה לא חדשים בימות החמה
ולא שחקים בעונת הגשמים
אלא נותן לה כלים של חמישים זוז בימות הגשמים
והיא מתכסה בבלאותיהן בימות החמה
והשחקים שלה
נותן לה מאה כסף לצורכה ואוכלת עמו מלילי שבת
ללילי שבת
ואם אין נותן לה מעה כסף לצורכה
מעשה ידיה שלה
ומה היא עושה לו
משקל חמש סלעים שתי ביהודה
שהן עשר סלעים בגליל עשר סלעים ערב ביהודה

שהן עשרים סלעים בגליל
ואם היתה מניקה פוחתין לה ממעשי ידיה
ומוסיפין לה על מזונותיה
במה דברים אמורים בעני שבישראל
אבל מכובד הכל לפי כבודו

> If a man maintains his wife through a trustee,
> he must give her [every week] not less than two kabs of wheat or four kabs of barley.
> Said R. Jose: "Only R. Ishmael who lived near Edom granted her a supply of barley."
> He must also give her half a kab of pulse and half a log of oil and a kab of dried figs or a maneh of pressed figs.
> And if he has no [such fruit] he must supply her with a corresponding quantity of other fruit.
> He must also provide her with a bed, a mattress, and a rush mat.
> He must also give her [once a year] a cap for her head and a girdle for her loins;
> shoes [he must give her] each major festival;
> and clothing of the value of fifty zuz every year.
> She is not to be given new clothes in the summer or worn-out clothes in the winter,
> but must be given the clothing [of the value] of fifty zuz during the winter,
> and she clothes herself with them when they are worn out during the summer;
> and the worn-out clothes remain her property.
> He must also give her [even] a silver ma'ah (coin) for her other requirements.
> She is to eat with him on the night of every Sabbath.
> If he does not give her [even] a silver ma'ah (coin) for her other requirements,
> her handiwork belongs to her.
> What [is the quantity of work that] she gets from him?
> The weight of five selas of warp which amounts to ten selas in Galilee.
> Weight of ten selas of woof in Judaea amounts to twenty selas in Galilee.
> If she is nursing [her child] her handiwork is reduced and her maintenance is increased.
> All this applies to the poorest in Israel,
> but in the case of men of the better classes,
> all is fixed according to the dignity of his position.

The explanation at the end makes it clear that while it relates to the poorest in Israel, for others the allowance is fixed according to the husband's status.

Since the food list does not mention wine, it would seem that poor men who provided for their wives through a third party did not have to give them wine. Indeed, the beraita in the Tosefta Ketubot (chap. 5,

Halakhah 7) says so specifically: "She does not have wine because the wives of the poor do not drink." Both Babylonian and Jerusalem Talmuds establish a link between this Mishnah and the debate over women's wine allowances.

The debate in the Babylonian Talmud starts with a general statement relying on the Mishnah, "Wine is not awarded to a woman."

The Jerusalem Talmud, like the beraita and possibly based on it, states, "She has no wine because poor women in Israel do not drink wine."

In the Jerusalem Talmud (chap. 5, Halakhah 11), the debate unfolds simply and clearly. As evidence that wives of rich men do drink wine, there is the story of Martha daughter of Beithos, to whom "a judgment of two measures of wine a day were awarded."[1] The reaction of the Talmud is astonishment ("And the courts award wine?") on the basis of the established verdict "Wine is not awarded to women."

This well-known verdict is explained by R. Hiyya bar Adda's statement: "Whoring, wine, and the juice of the grape steal the heart."[2] The astonishment is explained in two ways:

a. through the words of R. Joshua son of Levi, relying on the last Mishnah clause that awards wine to nursing mothers because it increases their milk, and one may assume that he justified Martha daughter of Beithos on that basis;[3]

b. through the words of R. Hezekiah from R. Abbahu from R. Johanan, who explained that the wine awarded to Martha daughter of Beithos was for her cooking.[4]

---

[1]The story of Martha daughter of Beithos, to whom the Sages awarded two se'ot of wine a day, is also in the midrash Aichah Rabbati, A50, with an addition: "when Joshua her husband died." The development takes the path of the Jerusalem Talmud discussion. By contrast "Thus it is taught," indicating a beraita, introduces "Wine is not awarded to a woman." The beraita is expounded by R. Hiyya bar Abba: "because of whoring, as it is said, whoring, wine, and strong drink steal away the heart." In reply, R. Hezekiah and R. Abbahu in the name of R. Johanan stated "for her cooking." Moreover, R. Joshua b. Levi interprets the Mishnah: "and it is also taught, if she is nursing, her handiwork is reduced, and her maintenance is increased, and the Rabbi Yehoshua ben Levi said, 'Whence an increase in wine, because wine increases the milk.'"

[2]The judgment in the Babylonian Talmud is given as that of the Eretz Israel Amora, R. Eleazar, and in the Jerusalem Talmud without the Amora's name. However, R. Hiyya bar Adda, who interprets it, may be, from the parallel in the Midrash Aichah Rabbati, Rabbi Hiyya bar Abba who was a disciple of R. Eleazar. The Leyden manuscript version's Hiyya bar Adda contradicts this.

[3]In the Babylonian Talmud nursing could not be the explanation, since she was awaiting the levir's decision.

[4]Relates to a widow, not to a woman under her husband's authority.

Thus the section of the Jerusalem Talmud relating to our discussion:

יין אין לה שאין עניות ישראל שותות יין
ועשירות שותות והתני מעשה במרתא בת בייתוס
שפסקו לה חכמים סאתיים יין בכל יום
ובית דין פוסקים יין?
אמר רבי חייא בר אדא על שום זנות יין ותירוש יקח לב
והא תנינן אם היתה מניקה פוחתין לה מעשה ידיה ומוסיפים לה על מזונותיה
מה מוסיף?
רבי יהושע בן לוי אמר יין שהוא מרבה את החלב
רבי חזקיה בן רבי אבהו בשם רבי יוחנן
אף לתבשיליה פסקו
אף על פי כן קללה אותן ואמרה להן כך תתנו לבנותיכם
אמר ר אחא וענינו אחריה אמן

> She does not have wine because poor women in Israel do not drink wine.
> Rich women do, as did Martha daughter of Beithos
> to whom the Sages awarded two se'ahs of wine a day.
> And do the courts award wine?
> Said R. Hiyya bar Adda because whoring, wine, and strong drink steal away the heart.
> But we have learned that if she is nursing, her handiwork is decreased and her maintenance is increased.
> What is increased?
> R. Joshua b. Levi said wine, because it increases the supply of milk.
> R. Hezekiah b. R. Abbahu stated in the name of R. Johanan that wine was awarded for her cooking.
> Even so, she cursed them saying, may you grant such allowances to your daughters.
> And R. Abbahu said we replied Amen after her.

In this Eretz Israel source there are two different concepts as regards awarding a wine allowance to women. The first (apparently of R. Eleazar, as it appears from the debate in the Babylonian Talmud) is that women should not be awarded wine at all, since it affects their sexual behavior adversely.

The second is that rich women should be awarded wine, since this is a matter of wealth or status, unconnected to women's behavior. By contrast with the Jerusalem Talmud, the text in the Babylonian Talmud builds on but one concept—that wine is not awarded to women because of its effect on their sexual behavior. That concept links different sources in the discussion in a tenuous and at times startling manner.

Careful comparison of the Babylonian and Jerusalem Talmud discussions, and study of the stories at the end of the former, lead to one conclusion: that the editor of the collection, who placed it at the end of

Women and Wine

the debate, had his own view, different from and even opposed to the one expressed in the legal judgments reported in the discussion.

The discussion that is overtly intended to establish and prove that "Wine allowances are not awarded to women" is in fact undermined by the collection of stories that follow it. This expresses, both through the content of the individual stories and by the way they are arranged, a different concept, familiar from the beraita in the Jerusalem Talmud: poor women do not drink wine but wealthy women do.

Thus the negotiation in the Babylonian Talmud:

נותן לה חצי קב קטנית.
ואילו יין לא קתני
מסייע ליה לר׳ אלעזר דאמר ר׳ אלעזר
אין פוסקין יינות לאישה ואם תאמר
"אלכה אחרי מאהבי נותני לחמי ומימי צמרי
ופשתי שמני ושיקויי"
דברים שהאישה משתוקקת עליהן
ומאי נינהו? תכשיטין
דרש רבי יהודה איש כפר נבוריא*
ואמרי לה איש כפר ** נפור חיל
מנין שאין פוסקין יינות לאישה?
שנאמר "ותקם חנה אחרי אכלה בשילה ואחרי שתה"
שתה ולא שתת אלא מעתה אכלה ולא אכל הכי נמי!
אנן מדשני קרא בדיבוריה קאמרינן
מכדי בגוה קא עסיק ואתי מאי טעמא שני?
ש׳מ שתה ולא שתת
מתיבי רגילה נותנין לה!
רגילה שאני, דאמר רב חיננא בר כהנא אמר שמואל
רגילה נותנין לה כוס אחד
שאינה רגילה נותנין לה שתי כוסות
מאי קאמר?
אמר אביי הכי קאמר: רגילה בפני בעלה שתי כוסות
שלא בפני בעלה נותנין לה כוס אחד
אינה רגילה בפני בעלה אלא כוס אחד, שלא בפני בעלה אין נותנין לה כל עקר.
ואי בעית אימא רגילה נותנין לה לציקי קדרה
דא׳ר אבהו א׳ר יוחנן
מעשה בכלתו של נקדימון בן גוריון
שפסקו לה חכמים סאתים יין***
לציקי קדרה מערב שבת לערב שבת
אמרה להן: כך תפסקו לבנותיכם
תנא שומרת יבם היתה ולא ענו אחריה אמן.
תנא כוס אחד יפה לאישה, שניים נוול הוא
שלשה תובעת בפה

ארבעה אפילו חמור תובעה בשוק ואינה מקפדת*****
אמר רבא ולא שנו אלא שאין בעלה עמה, אבל בעלה עמה לית לן בה*****
והא חנה דבעלה עמה הוא!
אכסנאי שאני דאמר רב הונא מנין לאכסנאי שאסור בתשמיש המטה?
שנאמר: "וישכימו בבוקר וישתחוו לפני ה'
וישובו ויבאו אל ביתם הרמתה וידע אלקנה את חנה אשתו ויזכרה ה' "
השתא אין מעיקרא לא.

---

*RB: Navraya; RC: Govrana; LF: Nevoraya; H1: Giboraya; H2: Navorya.
**RC: ish Gibor (a hero); RB, H2: ish Navor; LF: navor (and perhaps a hero); H1, H3, HP: a hero.
***M: two hundred zuz.
****M: Even if an ass solicits her in the streets, she does not care. RB: Even if an ass in the streets solicits her, she does not care.
***** HP: her husband keeps her; LF: her husband hides her.

The man must also give her half a kab of pulse.
Wine, however, is not mentioned.
This provides support for a view of R. Eleazar. For R. Eleazar stated [65a]:
No allowance for wine is made for a woman. And you should point out the scriptural text, 'I will go after my lovers, that give me my bread and my water, my wool and my flax, my oil and my drink'
[it may be replied that the reference is to] things which a woman desires. And what are they? Jewelry.
R. Judah of Kefar Nabiryah (others say of Kefar Napor Hayil) made the following exposition:
Whence is it derived that no allowance for wines is made for a woman?
[From Scripture in which it is said], 'So Hannah rose up after she had eaten in Shiloh, and after drinking,' only 'he had drunk' but she did not drink.
Now, then, would you also [interpret] 'She had eaten' that he did not eat?
What we say is [that the deduction may be made] because the text has deliberately been changed.
For consider: It was dealing with her, why did it change [the form]? Consequently it may be deduced that it was 'he who drank' and that she did not drink.
An objection was raised: If [a woman] is accustomed [to drink] she is given [an allowance of drink]!—where she is accustomed to drink the case is different.
For R. Hinena b. Kahana stated in the name of Samuel,
'If she was accustomed [to drink] she is given an allowance of one cup;
if she was not accustomed [to it] she is given an allowance of two cups.'
What does he mean?

Abaye replied: 'It is this that he means: If she was in the habit [of drinking] two cups in the presence of her husband she is given one cup in his absence;
If she is used [to drink] in the presence of her husband only one cup, she is given none at all in his absence. And if you prefer I might say: If she is used [to drink] she is allowed some wine for her puddings only.'
For R. Abbahu stated in the name of R. Johanan: It happened that when the Sages granted the daughter-in-law of R. Nakdimon b. Gorion
a weekly allowance of two se'ahs for her puddings she said to them,
'May you grant such allowances to your daughters.'
A Tanna taught: She was a woman awaiting the decision of the levir. Hence they did not reply Amen after her.
A Tanna taught: one cup is becoming to a woman; two are degrading
[and if she has] three she solicits publicly
[but if she has] four she solicits even an ass in the street and cares not.
Rava said: 'This was taught only [in respect of a woman] whose husband is not with her. But if her husband is with her [the objection to her drinking] does not arise.'
But surely [there is the case of] Hannah whose husband was with her!
With a guest it is different; for R. Huna stated, Whence is it inferred that a guest is forbidden marital union?
[From Scripture in] which it is said, 'And they rose up in the morning early and worshipped before the Lord,
and returned, and came to their house to Ramah; and Elkanah knew Hannah his wife; and the Lord remembered her,' only then but not before.

The debate begins by maintaining that the Mishnah supports R. Eleazar who said, "Wine allowances are not awarded to women." A possible contradiction is introduced by a verse from Hosea,[5] and rejected immediately. Then comes a quotation from R. Judah of Kefar Nabiryah,[6]

---

[5] The contradiction is most puzzling because literally "I will go after my lovers, that give me...my drink" seems to indicate that the woman's thoroughly reprehensible desire is for drink, and for lovers. It follows that there is no need at all for an explanation, based on the similarity of the Hebrew words, that 'drink' is something the woman longs for, like jewels, in order to resolve the contradiction, because no contradiction exists.

[6] Nabiryah: This village is mentioned several times in the Talmud and the Midrashim. Klein in *Eretz Hagalil*, p. 132, identifies it with Navaritim, 4 km. northeast of Safad, whose ruins include an ancient synagogue. Rabbi Judah of Kfar Nabiryah is also mentioned in Megillah (18a). "Rabbi Judah of Kefar Nabiryah, or as some say, of Kefar Gibbor Hayil, gave the following homily: What is meant by the verse 'For the silence is praise'? (Psalm 65). The best of all drugs is silence." The translation is according Rashi's interpretation.

who bases "Wine allowances are not awarded to women" on Samuel 1:9, "So Hannah rose up after she had eaten in Shiloh, and after drinking." Having proved the point, so to speak, about wine allowances and women by means of the Mishnah and by interpreting the biblical text, a contradiction comes in the beraita that states, "If she is used to it, it is given to her."

The contradiction is rejected on grounds that "one who is accustomed" is different. Here commences a long parenthetical statement in which the claim is supported by the statement of Hinena bar Kahana in the name of Samuel. The statement itself ends with the astonishing sentence, "If she was not accustomed, she is given an allowance of two cups." This is interpreted by a statement of Abaye.[7] Further on come alternative grounds: "If she is accustomed, it is granted to her for her puddings."[8]

These arguments are reinforced by the story of the daughter-in-law of Rav Nakdimon son of Gorion, which appears to be the same as the story of Martha daughter of Beithos,[9] cited in the Jerusalem Talmud and

---

[7] Abaye's saying does not correspond with the ending of Samuel, who said, "If she is not accustomed, she is awarded two cups." The Tosafot beginning with "is not" explain that if she is not accustomed to having two cups in the presence of her husband, but only one, in his absence she gets none at all. This last clause, however, is an addition to Samuel's own words.

[8] Rashi, First Edition (Shitah Mekubetzet), states that this justification is based on Samuel's words and not on the beraita "If she is accustomed, she is awarded it," as the Tosaphot. Following this line of argument, one understands Samuel thus: If she is accustomed, she is awarded one cup for her cooking, since one suspects that if she gets more, she will get drunk, for she is used to drinking wine. At the same time, one who is not used to drinking wine is awarded two cups for her cooking, because there is no suspicion that she will get drunk on the rest. From the foregoing it appears that "If you want, you can say 'If she is accustomed she is awarded [wine] for her cooking'" is in essence an alternative to understanding Abaye's saying as an interpretation of Samuel.

[9] The entire story is presented as R. Abbahu's, in the name of R. Jochanan, while in the Jerusalem Talmud and in the Midrash, R. Jochanan merely explains: "for their cooking." This is to justify the contradiction between the story and the ruling that wine is not awarded to women. Avot d'Rabbi Nathan (A, chap. 6; B, chap. 13) presents a story of Nakdimon b. Gorion's daughter, who spent "a golden dinar from one Sabbath eve to the next on her cooking." Possibly the story in our discussion is based on this one, as the expression "from one Sabbath eve to the next" seems to be taken from it. Thus a story unrelated to wine allowances, but otherwise suitable to the purpose, has been worked into the discussion. The woman's reaction, given in the Jerusalem Talmud story, "[She] cursed them and said, 'May you grant such allowances to your daughters,'" shows that she considered the wine allotment very small. This reinforces the explanation that the Babylonian Talmud's story deliberately specified a smaller amount, taken, it seems, from another story, "From Sabbath eve to Sabbath eve."

in Midrash in Aichah Rabati. The discussion ends with the beraita, "One cup is becoming for a woman, two are degrading, with three she solicits publicly, with four she solicits even an ass in the street and cares not." Rava interprets the beraita to refer to a woman whose husband is not with her. An attempt is made to reject this with the verse from Samuel 1, said to prove that Hannah did not drink wine even though her husband was with her. This in turn was disproved by maintaining that Hannah and her husband were in the special circumstances of wayfarers, so that she did not drink.[10]

The final conclusion from this part of the discussion is that a wine allowance is not awarded to a woman whose husband is not with her, and even if she was accustomed to drinking wine with her husband, she is awarded only a very small amount of wine for her puddings.

Following the debate through the Babylonian Talmud up to this point reveals the concept that a woman should not be allowed to drink wine in the absence of her husband, since wine affects her sexual behavior adversely. Her self-control is unreliable, and hence she requires patronage and supervision.

This section moves away from the theme of the Mishnah, which deals only with poor men's wives who are provided for by a trustee. It either ignores or does not know[11] the beraita "She has no wine because poor women in Israel do not drink wine."

The discussion affirms the general statement "Wine allowances are not awarded to women" by approving it with very narrow reservations: a minimal amount for women accustomed to it, and perhaps even this is to be used only for cooking.

The beraita at the end of the negotiation is extreme as regards the changes in women's behavior as a result of drinking. Following it is a discussion that affirms and reinforces this position by stating that a woman is allowed to drink wine only in the presence of her husband and in her own home. Introducing this beraita and Rava's explanation at this point in the discussion highlights the rationale for the generalization. Wine allowances are not to be awarded to women who are not under their husbands' supervision:[12] women are "the weaker sex" and drinking

---

[10]The beraita and the discussion are in Khallah Rabbati (chap. 2, Halakhah 8) as well. The only difference is that there the interpretation "a woman whose husband is not with her" is not in the name of Rava.

[11]See Hanoch Albeck, *Mekharim be-beraita u-va-Tosephta ve-yakhasam le-Talmud*, (Jerusalem, 1944), p. 115.

[12]The explanation that drinking wine makes women lose sexual control is found in several places in the Talmud. In Berachot (63a) and in Sotah (2a), a baraita explains why Nazir follows Sotah, teaching that "Whoever witnesses a suspected woman in her disgrace should withhold himself from wine." The Mishnah, Sotah

wine breaks down their self-control, necessitating supervision and control.

The position in the first part of the Babylonian Talmud debate is "Wine allowances are not awarded to women." This is not limited to chap. 1, states that when a wayward woman was brought before the High Court in Jerusalem she was warned "My daughter, wine does much, frivolity does much, youth does much, bad neighbors do much."

At the same time, the Talmud contains many sayings about men drinking wine. It is not censured, and often recommended, with some instances of restrictions for certain people, or while performing designated duties: e.g., "One sort of person drinks wine with good results, another sort drinks wine with disastrous results. A student of the Sages drinks (their advice) with good results; an ignoramus drinks (the advice of Sages and ignores it) with disastrous results" (Jerusalem Talmud, Ma'aser Sheni chap. 4, Halakhah 6). Or "He who drinks a quarter [measure] of wine does not teach," and from what follows, this appears to relate to one unused to drinking. The attitude to women, then, is like the attitude to ignorant men, or worse. The differences are evident from a comparison of two sets of sources. One discusses the process of inebriation in the male, from Tanhuma (Noah 13) and Yalkut Shimoni (Noah 61). The other discusses the process in females and comes from the beraita in our Babylonian Talmud discussion, in Khallah Rabbati and in Ketubot:

Midrash Tanhuma	Yalkut Shimoni	Kallah Rabbati, Ketubot
Before a man drinks of the wine he is innocent as a lamb. The ignoramus who drinks heartily is bold as a lion and says, there is no one like me in the world.	When a man drinks one cup of wine he is like a lamb, modest and humble like a lamb before her shearers.	One cup is becoming to a woman.
	When he drinks two cups he becomes bold as a lion and starts bragging and says, who is like me?	Two are degrading to her.
When he drinks too much he becomes like a pig: he soils himself with urine and other filth.	When he drinks three or four he becomes like a pig.	If she has three, she solicits publicly. With four even if an ass solicits her in the street, she cares not.

The difference between the sexes is clear: A man's conduct changes from modesty to exaggerated self-confidence to playing the fool and to self-debasement, not necessarily in the sexual domain. With the second glass, however, a woman's conduct changes at once to self-debasement then to complete loss of specifically sexual control. The idea of these differing effects of wine appears to arise from the perception of women as irresponsible sexual creatures who have to be controlled and protected from their surroundings and from themselves. This seems to be the basis of R. Eleazar's saying that good advice is not sufficient for women as it is for men, but they must be watched over by law. From that also follows the difference the Babylonian Talmud makes between a woman whose husband is with her, and one whose husband is not.

poor women, or those provided for by a third party, but applies to all women, poor or rich, wives or widows. The efforts of the Babylonian Talmud up to this point appear to advance the extreme view but actually complicate it. Some of the difficulties in the discussion seem to me to be the result of these efforts.

(a). The discussion opens with "wine is not mentioned in the Mishnah." Thus the Mishnah supports R. Eleazar, who said, "Wine is not allowed to *women*." It can be interpreted to mean merely poor married women provided for by a trustee, since only this group is discussed in the Mishnah list of provisions.

The Mishnah does not discuss women living with their husbands, or rich women provided for by a third party, or widows, poor or rich. The generalization is therefore false.

(b). R. Judah of Kefar Nabiryah's interpretation that bases the generalization "Wine is not allowed to women" on Samuel 1:9, "So Hannah rose up after she had eaten in Shiloh, and after she had drunk," is bewildering to say the least. Hannah is a married woman living with her husband, as the discussion itself mentions further on, while "is not allowed" refers to the court. This shows that "Wine is not awarded to a woman" refers to one who does not live with her husband. (Indeed, in the source quoted to contradict the interpretation, it is said, "If she is accustomed it is given" by the husband, and not, if she is accustomed it is *awarded*, by the courts.)

(c). It appears that in the Gemara discussion on the question "If she is accustomed, it is given to her," the justification and its reinforcement refer to the woman who lives with her husband and only Abaye returns the discussion to its original theme. Rava also finds it necessary to state, "This was taught only in respect to a woman whose husband is not with her."

Several passages of this specific discussion are complicated and difficult, apparently because various sources that mention awarding a wine allowance to women not living with their husbands have been brought together, even though they discuss different matters.

Conspicuous among the difficulties are:

1. "If she is accustomed it is given to her" is brought in as a Tannaitic source. However, no beraita or Mishnah makes precisely this statement. Possibly this is merely a truncated quotation from Samuel, brought in as a Tannaitic statement to contradict the Mishnah.

2. The assumption in the question is bewildering since in the source, brought in as a basis for the discussion, she who is "accustomed" is set apart from other women. Why, then, should

the Gemara ask about the woman who is accustomed to it, and then answer the question by saying that she who is accustomed is different?[13]

3. Samuel's explanations, brought in to highlight the distinction between those accustomed and those unaccustomed, are in themselves surprising. It is unclear why "she who is unaccustomed is given two cups." Thus Samuel seems to refer to a woman whose husband gives her wine, and not to a court judgment relating to wine for a woman living alone.

4. Taking Abaye's statements as an explanation for Samuel's is not entirely logical, because Abaye's words are not found in Samuel's. True, by stretching the point, Samuel's "the woman who is unaccustomed is given two cups" can be understood as "and she is unaccustomed to be given two cups." But according to this understanding, the law "She is not given anything" is missing. It is more plausible that Abaye is trying to return the discussion to the original subject: awarding wine to a woman in her husband's absence.

(d) The story of Nakdimon son of Gorion's daughter, introduced to strengthen the position that wine is awarded even to women accustomed to it, for their cooking only, appears to combine two or even three stories, two of which are not even related to the issue of awarding wine to women (see note 9). Nakdimon son of Gorion's daughter, who was awarded a golden dinar for her cooking needs from Sabbath eve to Sabbath eve, is cited also in Avoth d'Rabi Nathan (version a in chap. 6; version b in chap. 13). The story may have been introduced into the discussion as if it related to a wine allowance, to show that even to rich women accustomed to wine, it was granted by the courts only for their cooking, and in small amounts.

In the discussion in the Jerusalem Talmud and in Midrash Aichah Rabati, as stated previously, the story is about Martha daughter of Beithos, who was awarded *two cups of wine a day*. There is no mention of wine for cooking. The idea of wine for cooking in the Gemara is R. Hezekiah's explanation of the story, not a part of the story itself.

---

[13]The Tosaphot beginning with "I am accustomed" show this by stating: "And if so, what proof is needed?" The beraita itself, when it states "is accustomed," is justified by explaining that R. Eleazar also meant those who were accustomed to wine. The Gemara thus distinguishes between two groups of those who are accustomed (like Abaye's distinction between one used to two cups and one used to one).

The difficulties in the discussion, then, would seem to have emerged out of the tendency to support R. Eleazar's judgment "Wine is not awarded to a woman," and to link it to the effect they assumed wine to have on women's sexual behavior.

Hence the opening argument, to the effect that the Mishnah supports R. Eleazar's categorical judgment, "Wine is not awarded to women." The Mishnah itself, however, taken literally, does not support this at all.[14] The same influence is brought in R. Judah of Kefar Nabiryah's commentary on Samuel 1 in a way that supports R. Eleazar, even though the biblical text is about a woman who was with her husband.

The next section includes the statement "given to the woman accustomed to it," in contradiction to the conclusion drawn from the Mishnah.

The contradiction is resolved by assuming that one who is accustomed is different. Samuel's statement is then introduced in affirmation. Finally the question "What did he mean?" presents Abaye's words in explanation of Samuel's statement. This whole section is confused and difficult, due entirely to the attempt to support R. Eleazar.

Hence "given to the woman accustomed to it," presented as a contradiction, may have been taken from a purposely truncated statement of Samuel's. Then the problem is "resolved" by "one accustomed is different," followed by Samuel's full statement in justification of the so-called solution. Since direct understanding of the text does not support the "solution," Abaye's strained explanation is introduced: with great effort this returns the discussion to the woman whose husband is not with her. Then comes another solution, "She who is accustomed is given [wine] for her cooking." The story of Nakdimon son of Gorion's daughter, originally quite unrelated to wine judgments, is brought in as further support.

The entire negotiation, including the spurious contradiction negated in two alternative ways, with forced support brought in for each, is all a matter of supporting R. Eleazar's "Wine is not awarded to women" and showing how all-embracing and decisive it is. Moreover, including the beraita on what wine does to a woman at the end of the negotiation further directs the debate on the issue of women and wine.

An understanding of the negotiation section in the Babylonian Talmud discussion reveals just how far it differs from its parallel in the Jerusalem Talmud.

---

[14]Possibly the author of the Gemara himself felt that. Otherwise there was no point in adding the words of R. Judah of Kfar Nabiryah about the supporting homily.

At the end of the Jerusalem source, wine is awarded to women only because they are nursing, or for cooking, even though the Gemara itself distinguishes between poor women not accustomed to drinking wine in their husbands' houses, and rich women who are.[15] There is even the example of the rich widow, Martha daughter of Beithos, to whom the Sages awarded wine.

Indeed elsewhere in the Jerusalem Talmud (Ketubot chap. 11, Halakhah 1, 34a) it is explicitly stated that "A widow has wine," which seems to refer to a wealthy widow accustomed to it when she lived with her husband. In the Jerusalem Talmud, then, we find an economic direction, unlike the behavior-related direction of the Babylonian Talmud: the distinction is made between rich and poor women, and not between women and men, as in the Babylonian Talmud.

In the second section of the discussion in the Babylonian Talmud we find a collection of three stories about women who petitioned for a judgment relating to wine. The contents of the individual stories, their arrangement in the collection and the links between them hint at a tendency quite different from the one in the negotiation in the first section of the discussion, and one very close to the position of the Jerusalem Talmud.

Looking at each individual story, we note their common features and the significance of the links that connect them:

חומה דביתהו דאביי
אתאי לקמיה דרבא
אמרה ליה פסוק לי מזוני פסק לה
פסוק לי חמרא
א״ל ידענא ביה בנחמני דלא הוה שתי* חמרא
אמרה ליה חיי דמר
דהוה משקי ליה בשופרזי״* כי האי
בהדי דקא מחוא ליה איגלי דרעא
נפל נהורא בבי דינא
קם רבא על לביתיה
תבעה לבת רב חסדא
אמרה ליה בת רב חסדא
מאן הוי האידנא בבי דינא?
אמר חומא דביתהו דאביי
נפקא אבתרה מחתא לה בקולפי דשידא

---

[15] As to the link between wealth and the custom of wine drinking, Moshe Ber in *Amora'i Bavel, Perakim be-hayyei ha-khalkhalah*, p. 323 cites the story of Homa, Abaye's wife from our discussion, as an example that we cannot always rely solely on an economic explanation. Abaye was unused to wine in the home of his uncle, Rava, so even afterward, when he became head of a yeshiva and his economic situation improved, he did not drink wine.

Women and Wine

עד דאפקה מכולי מחוזא***
אמרה לה
קטלת ליך תלתא
ואתת למיקטל אחרינא?

---

* RB, H3, HP: "did not give you wine to drink."
** RC: "by the life of my master, he gave me the best wine to drink."
*** M adds: "out of the academy" (and out of Mehuza).

> Homa, Abaye's wife, came to Rava and asked him,
> "Grant me an allowance of board," and he granted her the allowance.
> "Grant me [she again demanded] an allowance of wine."
> "I know," he said to her, "that Nahmani did not drink wine."
> "By the life of the Master [I swear]," she replied,
> "that he gave me to drink from horns like this."
> As she was showing it to him her arm was uncovered
> And a light shone upon the court.
> Rava rose, went home and solicited R. Hisda's daughter (his wife).
> "Who was at the court today?" enquired R. Hisda's daughter.
> "Homa the wife of Abaye," he replied.
> Thereupon she followed her, striking her with the straps of a chest until she chased her out of all Mahuza.
> "You have," she said to her, "already killed three [men], and now you are out to kill another!"

The first story tells of Homa, widow of Abaye, who came before Rava and asked for a wine allowance. Rava refused on the grounds that "I know Nahmani did not drink wine." From here on the story takes a dramatic turn unrelated to women and wine allowances. To convince Rava that she was accustomed to drinking wine she displays her arm to show the size of the "horns"[16] into which her husband poured her wine. The evil inclination overcame Rava at the sight of her fair arm, and he went home and demanded that his wife come to bed.

She, ascertaining that her husband's baser instincts had been roused by Homa, beat her with the straps of a chest and ran her out of Mahuza, so that Homa would no longer display her beauty there and cause the death of another man, besides her three deceased husbands, related in Yebamot 64b.

Returning to our discussion, from what Homa told Rava, "My husband gave me to drink from horns like this," from what the daughter of R. Hisda told Homa, and from what Yebamot 64b relates of Abaye and

---

[16] According to the Aruch, *shufrazini* comes from the Arabic, 'a large cup', and from this the word *shefer zeini*, 'an elongated glass drinking vessel', evolved. In the opening, *shufraza*, the writer theorizes that the origin may lie in an Arabic word meaning 'a large plate': s. *shufraz*, pl. *shufrazey* .

Homa, it is clear that she is a widow asking for wine from her support allowance and her marriage contract.

From Rava's answer, it appears that he thought that wine was not awarded to a widow unused to drinking wine in her husband's house, although the Mishnah has no law on this specific point. (Our Mishnah deals with a married woman living separately, not with a widow.)

From the argument between Rava and Homa, clearly the decision to grant her a wine allowance depended on economic considerations or on her previous life style. The central question was the standard of living to which she had been accustomed in her husband's house.

In Shabbat (33a) Rava indicates the same familiarity when talking of Abaye: "We knew that Nahmani abstained from drink." In Berachot (42b) R. Isaac bar Joseph, visiting at Abaye's home on a holiday, noticed that he said the blessing over every glass of wine. Said he to him, "With all due respect, do you not think like Joshua son of Levi?" (that on Sabbaths and holidays, blessing the wine before the meal eliminates the need to do so at the end). "I am considering the matter," he answered. Rashi explains the response as "I am not used to ending a meal with wine." From these sources it is clear that Abaye was not used to rich meals, a fact certainly known to Rava.

A reproof to the widow who wants to raise her standard of living may be inferred from his familiar tone. And her reply, "My husband gave me to drink in horns like this," may be understood as a protest against Rava, for the insulting insinuation that she lived in poverty in Abaye's home.[17] However, as Behr maintains (note 15), the habit of drinking wine may not have been related only to economic status, and Abaye's household may not have been used to drinking wine even when he became well off.

In any case, it is clear in this story that Rava's decision is determined by the customs and patterns of consumption in her husband's home. This consideration is very close to the law stated in the Tosephta and the Jerusalem Talmud, "Poor women in Israel do not drink wine." From the end of the incident in court, it may be understood that Rava did not award a wine allowance, since it would have been mentioned had he done so.

The second story tells of the wife of Rav Joseph, Rava's son, who asked R. Nehemiah (according to the RIF's version, she asked Rav

---

[17]Tosaphot Rid contains another version: "We know that in Nahmani's home wine was not poured out in *shufrazi* and she replied 'on your life, he gave me wine in *shufrazi* this big.'" Indeed manuscripts RB and RC, and *Hagadot Hazal* contain the words משקי ליך which mean 'give you drink', instead of שתי meaning 'drinks'.

Joseph) to award her support and wine. He complies and explains, "We know that people in Mehuza drink wine." Here is the story in literal translation:

דביתהו דרב יוסף בריה דרבא
אתאי לקמיה דרב נחמיה בריה דרב יוסף*
אמרה ליה פסוק לי מזוני
פסק לה
פסוק לי חמרא
פסק לה
אמר לה: ידענא בהו בבני מחוזה דשתו חמרא

---

*LF: "came before Rav Joseph to Pumpaditah."

> The wife of Rav Joseph the son of Rava
> came before R. Nehemiah the son of Rav Joseph
> and said to him, "Grant me an allowance of board,"
> and he granted her.
> "Grant me also an allowance of wine," and he granted her.
> "I know," he said to her, "that people of Mehuza drink wine."

Mehuza people used to get drunk at their feasts, according to Taanit 27a. It seems abundantly clear then that a wine allowance was awarded to the woman in the story because she was known to be well-off, and because of her habits of consumption during her married life.

The third story tells of the widow of Rav Joseph son of Rav Menashya of Dewil who came before Rav Joseph. From her blunt answer at the end it is clear that she is a widow. Here is the story in its own words:

דביתהו דרב יוסף בריה דרב מנשיא מדויל*
אתי לקמיה דרב יוסף
א'ל פסוק לי מזוני
פסק לה
פסוק לי חמרא
פסק לה
פסוק לי שיראי
אמר לה
שיראי למה לך?
אמרה ליה
לך ולחברך ולחברורך

---

*M, RC: "of Dewil" is missing.

> The wife of R. Joseph, son of R. Menashya of Dewil
> came before R. Joseph and said to him,
> "Grant me an allowance of board,"

and he granted her.

"Grant me," she said "an allowance of wine," and he granted her.

"Grant me," she said again, "an allowance of silks."

"Why silks?" he asked. "For your sake," she replied, "and for the sake of your friend, and for the sake of your associates."

In this story the request for wine is granted without any need for her to justify it. The reason emerges later and it is economic. The woman then asks for silks, and this request is contested. Her sharp reply shows that the judge insulted her. Silken clothes were a luxury item even for rich women used to drinking wine.[18] Once again, a wine allowance was based purely and simply on the woman's financial status and her habits in her husband's home.

As for the order of the stories, they are not arranged according to an external technical criterion: not according to the name of the judge, nor to the person who reported the story, nor in chronological order. Rather it is the central theme of each story that determines the order.

The first story is about a woman who was not granted a wine allowance. The protagonist, Homa, lived during her marriage in a home where wine was not usually drunk, and hence it was not awarded to her as a widow.

The second story is about a woman, probably a widow, who was granted a wine allowance. She had lived with her husband in a home where wine was drunk as a matter of course, and hence when she was living alone she was awarded a wine allowance.

The third story is about a rich widow in whose case there was no doubt about the outcome of her request for a wine allowance. The protagonist when she was married lived in a very rich home, so there was no question about granting her wine as a widow.

Ordering the stories in this way shows the editor's intention of bringing the discussion back to its original point of departure, the Mishnah interpreted literally, from which the first part of the debate digressed; that is, it returns to the economic plane. The decision to grant wine allowances to widows is determined purely and simply by the standard of living and patterns of consumption in their husbands' homes.[19]

---

[18] In Ber, (ibid.) p. 324, we learn from this story that "silken clothes were a luxury even for women used to wine."

[19] Ber (ibid.) says that possibly the stories suggest a difference between an ordinary woman and a sage's wife, following the quotation from Berachot, end of 57a: "[Wine] is always good for a scholar." Obviously this distinction can be explained on the economic plane as well. However, even with this explanation, there is a difference between the Eretz Israel Amora, R. Eleazar, quoted in the

The approach in this latter part of the discussion resembles the one familiar to the Jerusalem Talmud. Here the law "Wine is not allowed to women" is not absolute and is not related to the woman's sexual conduct.

Placing the decision on the economic level puts the woman in a much more honorable position. She is not categorically forbidden to drink wine and is not a creature belonging to an inferior, childish sex. The judgment is not conditional to the husband's "supervision," but relates to her as a mature, responsible person.

Presenting the court judgment as a result of the woman's economic or social position fits in well with the Babylonian reality, in which wine was expensive and drinking it on weekdays signified higher economic status.[20]

In the earlier Eretz Israel debate, then, two systems find expression. The source of the first is Tannaitic material, in which there are rich women who are awarded wine allowances, even if only to improve their ability to nurse or to cook, and there are poor women who are not.

The second system is R. Eleazar's, although the Jerusalem Talmud does not mention him by name. It awards no wine allowances to women because wine has a bad effect on their sexual conduct.

In the first part of the discussion the Babylonian Talmud adopted the second system and built the negotiation around it, ignoring the first. However, in the second part, the collection of stories, we recognize the tendency to explain granting wine to women on the basis of economic status only.

Ending the debate with stories arranged as they are indicates an inclination to waive the behavior criterion in favor of the economic one.

In preferring the latter, the editor may have expressed the position that a wine allowance is no different from any other economic matter such as food and clothing. This may not be a great thing, because the wife is completely dependent on her husband in all matters economic. But it does indicate rejection of the patronizing position that holds that a woman must be supervised because she is an irresponsible, weak-minded creature.

Babylonian Talmud, "Wine is not awarded to a woman," i.e., any woman, and what may be inferred from the three stories. Ber himself stresses this.

[20]There are many proofs in Ber, (ibid.), pp. 318-324.

6

Mothers and Sons
(Babylonian Talmud Kidushin 30b-31a)

The debate in the Babylonian Talmud (Kidushin 30b) clarifies the Halakhah "All obligations of the father upon the son." After a short investigation of the subject comes a succession of beraitas, sayings, and stories connected with honoring one's father and mother. There are similar series in the Jerusalem Talmud in Kidushin (chap. 1, Halakhah 7) and in Peah (chap. 1, Halakhah 1).

The sayings and stories deal with the relationship of sons to parents: some are about the father-and-son relationship and others about the relationship between mother and son. We deal with the latter, of which there are four in the Babylonian Talmud, three appearing consecutively and the fourth standing alone as a sort of addendum to the stories of fathers and sons.

The parallel in the Jerusalem Talmud contains only two stories on mothers and sons. These appear together and are followed by sayings that relate to both as a single literary unit.

A comparative study of the mother-and-son stories in the Babylonian and Jerusalem Talmuds, both as to the content of individual stories and as to the collections, shows how the Eretz Israel stories were reworked in the Babylonian Talmud with an editorial purpose in mind. The editor wished to distinguish clearly between the relationships with each parent, and to point out the special characteristics of the son's relationship to his mother.

The first such story is that of Dama son of Nethinah and his mother. In the Babylonian Talmud it is appended to the stories about him and his father. The tales of this gentile from Ashkelon who was a shining example of honoring parents are given here in shortened form as R. Ulla's answer to the question "How far does honor to father and mother extend?" An extended version follows in R. Eliezer's answer. Following the two comes the moral of the story, and the response of R. Joseph. Then comes the story of Dama bar Nethinah and his mother, as told by Rav Dimi from Eretz Israel:

פעם אחת היה [דמא בן נתינה] לבוש סירקון של זהב
והיה יושב בין גדולי רומי
ובאתה אמו
וקרעתו ממנו
וטפחה לו על ראשו
וירקה לו בפניו
ולא הכלימה

> He [Dama son of Nethinah] was once wearing a gold embroidered silken cloak
> and sitting among Roman nobles,
> when his mother came,
> tore it off from him,
> struck him on the head,
> and spat in his face,
>   yet he did not shame her.

From this and the preceding stories, we do not know who Dama was, except for the fact that he was a gentile from Ashkelon. We do not know why he was sitting with the Roman council, nor why his mother behaved as she did.

It is interesting to compare this story with a parallel in two versions in the Jerusalem Talmud.[1]

Jerusalem Talmud Kidushin chap. 1, Halakhah 1	Jerusalem Talmud Peah chap. 1, Halakhah 7
כיבוד אב ואם רבי אבוה בשם רבי יוחנן (כתב יד וטיקן: רבי אבהו אמר בש' ר' יוחנן) שאלו את רי אליעזר (וטיקן: אלעזר) עד היכן כיבוד אב ואם אמר להן ולי אתן שואלין לכו שאלו את דמה בר נתינה דמה בן נתינה ראש פטרבולי הוה (וטיקן: פטרבולי היה)[3]	עד היכן הוא כיבוד אב ואם אמרו להן ולי אתן שואלין לכו שאלו לדמה בר נתינה (כ'' ליידן: ראש פטרבולי הוה)[2] פעם היתה אמו מסטרתו לפני בולי שלו ונפל קורדקסין שלה מידה והושיט לה כדי שלא תצטער

---

[1] The story appears in Devarim Rabbah (chap. 1, 15) as follows:
  The honoring of father and mother, how far does it extend? R. Abbahu said: "R. Eliezer the Great was asked by his disciples 'Can you give an example of (real) honoring of parents?' He replied: 'Go and see what Dama b. Nethinah at Ashkelon did. His mother was mentally afflicted, and she used to slap him in the presence of his colleagues, and all that he would say was: 'Mother, it is enough!'"

Mothers and Sons

פעם אחת היתה אמו מסטרתו
בפני כל בולי שלו (וטיקן: לפני)
ונפל קורקדין שלה מידה
והושיט לה (וטיקן: הושיטו)
כדי שלא תצטער. (וטיקן: אין 'כדי')

Honoring father and mother. R. Avuha in the name of R. Johanan: They asked R. Eliezer, How far does honor to parents extend?	To what extent does the requirement of honoring father and mother extend? He said to them: Are you asking me?
He said to them, are you asking me? Go ask Dama son of Nethinah, head of the patroboule.[3] Once his mother struck him in front of all his associates and her slipper fell from her hand. He gave it back to her so as not to shame her.	Go ask Dama son of Nethinah. (He was the chief at the patroboule of his town.)[2] One time his mother was slapping him before the entire council, and the slipper she was beating him with fell from her hand and he got down and gave it back to her so she would not be upset.

A comparison of the Babylonian story with the two versions from the Jerusalem Talmud reveals many differences.

(a) In the Jerusalem Talmud, Peah, R. Avuha in the name of R. Johanan, says that R. Eleazer was asked, "How far does honor to parents extend?" He replied with the story of Dama and his mother. In Kidushin the story is a reply to the same question, without mentioning who reported the question or who was asked. The story of Dama and his father is told in both places by R. Hezekiah as a separate story that paints a broad picture of Dama's character and of his fine conduct with his father and with people in general. By contrast, the Babylonian Talmud tells first "that R. Ulla was asked how far the honor to parents extends," and in the second instance (by Rav Judah in the name of Samuel) that the question was put to R. Eleazer. In both cases the answer was a much condensed version of the story of Dama bar Nethinah and his father, and the one about Dama and his mother is simply an addendum.

(b) In the Jerusalem Talmud stories Dama is described as the head of the patroboule while in the Babylonian Talmud he is simply "a certain pagan."

---

[2] The Aruch in the entries "pate" and "bul" explains that *pater* is Greek for 'father', from which derive 'patron' in Greek and Latin; *bul* in Greek and Syriac means 'counsel', also called 'counsel of the elders'. Hence *paterbuli* means 'chief judge' and the word ראש 'head' is a superfluous later addition.

[3] The Vatican manuscript, Peah, states simply "He was Pater Buli" without the word 'head'. This reinforces the Aruch interpretation, that it was a later addition not in the kernel story.

(c) In the Jerusalem Talmud no situation is depicted. It is simply stated that the event happened "in front of his associates." In the Babylonian Talmud, however, the situation is described at length: "Once he was wearing a gold embroidered silken cloak and sitting among Roman nobles."

(d) In the Jerusalem Talmud the incident with the mother is condensed: "Once his mother struck him." In the Babylonian Talmud it is described in detail and the mother's actions are arranged so as to follow an order of increasingly outrageous behavior: (1) his mother came, (2) tore (the cloak) from him, (3) struck him on the head, and (4) spat in his face.

(e) In the Jerusalem Talmud there is a detailed account of what the son did with the slipper, while the Babylonian Talmud simply states, "he did not shame her." According to the Midrash, which apparently follows the latter, he said nothing but "That's enough, Mother."

From the differences in (a) between the stories about Dama and his father in the two Talmuds, and the differences between the stories in the Babylonian Talmud itself, it appears that Sages in Babylon used Eretz Israel stories on the conduct of a wealthy gentile from Ashkelon, Dama son of Nethinah, toward his parents, as examples. The actual details of the stories were unknown and were not considered important.

(In the version of Rav Ulla the Sages were looking for goods, while in that of Rav Judah in the name of Samuel it was jewels for the ephod. In the latter version the Sages offered a reward of six hundred thousand golden dinars while in Rav Kahane's version it was eight hundred thousand.) The Sages in Babylon used condensed versions to teach the morals:[4] irrelevant details, like Dama son of Nethinah's identity and point of view, were left out.[5]

---

[4]The Kidushin discussion brings in shortened stories to teach how far honor to parents extends, while in Avodah Zarah (23a-24b) the shortened story is introduced to show internal contradiction in the words of R. Eleazar.

[5]The story of Dama ben Nethinah and his father appears in the Babylonian Talmud (Kidushin 30b-31a) thus:

> It was propounded of R. Ulla: "How far does the honor of parents (extend)?" He replied, "Go forth and see what a certain heathen, Dama son of Nethinah by name, did in Ashkelon. The Sages once desired merchandise from him, in which there was 600,000 (golden denarii) profit, but the key was lying under his father and so he did not trouble him."
>
> Rab Judah said in Samuel's name: "R. Eliezer was asked, 'How far does the honor of parents (extend)?' Said he: 'Go forth and see what a certain heathen, Dama son of Nethinah by name, did in Ashkelon. The Sages sought jewels for the ephod, at a profit of 600,000 (golden denarii)—R. Kahana taught: at a profit of 800,000—but as the key was lying under his father's pillow, he did not trouble him. The following year, the Holy One,

Mothers and Sons

Blessed be He, gave him his reward. A red heifer was born to him in his herd. When the Sages of Israel went to him (to buy it) he said to them: 'I know you, that (even) if I asked you for all the money in the world you would pay me. But I ask of you only the money which I lost through my father's honor!'"

In the Jerusalem Talmud, Kidushin 1, 7, and Peah 1, 1, the story is told thus:

Kidushin 1, 7	Peah 1, 1
Said R. Hezekiah, "He was a gentile from Ashkelon, and head of the *patroboule* of his town. Now if there was a stone on which his father had sat, he would never sit on it. When [his father] died, he made the stone into his god.	Said R. Hezekiah, "There was a gentile from Ashkelon [i.e., Dama ben Nethinah] who was chief of the *patroboule*." [He had so much respect for his father that] during his entire lifetime he never sat upon the stone seat upon which his father used to sit. [Furthermore] when his father died, he deemed the stone his god [in his father's honor].
Once Benjamin's jewel in the high priest's breastplate was lost [cf. Jastrow, p. 601]. They said, "Who has as fine a one as that?" They went to him and made a deal with him to buy it for a hundred dinars.	One time, the Jaspis-[stone] corresponding to the tribe of Benjamin [in the high priest's breastplate] was lost. [The Sages] said, "Does anyone have a gemstone like this? [If so, we can purchase it and replace the Jaspis]." Others replied, "Dama ben Nethinah has one like that." They went to him and agreed to pay him one hundred dinars.
He went to get it for them, and he found that his father was sleeping [on the box containing the jewel]. And some say the key to the box was on the finger of his father, and some say that his foot was stretched out over the box.	He went out to bring them the stone, and came upon his father who was sleeping. Some say the key to his jewelry box was attached to his father's finger. Others say his father's feet were resting on the jewelry box. [In either case, lest he disturb his father's sleep, Dama did not take the stone out of the box.] [Dama] returned and said to them, "I cannot bring the stone to you." [Misinterpreting Dama's actions, the Sages] said, "Perhaps he wants more money, [so] let us raise [our offer] to two hundred or maybe to a thousand dinars."
He went down to them and said, "I can't bring it to you." They raised the price to two hundred, then to a thousand. Once his father woke up from his sleep, he went up and got the jewel for them.	[Still] Dama would not bring them the stone, for fear of waking his father. When his father awoke from his slumber, [Dama] went and brought [the gem to the Sages].

They wanted to pay him what they had offered at the end, but he would not accept the money from them. He said, "Shall I sell you [at a price] the honor of my father?"	They wanted to give him the amount they last offered him, but he would not accept this [from them]. He said, "Now shall I sell you my father's honor for money? I will not make a profit at all from honoring my father!" [Dama therefore sold them the stone for the original price offered, one hundred dinars.]
How did the Holy One, blessed be He, reward him?	How did the Holy One, blessed be He, pay [Dama] a reward [for honoring his father in this way]? Said R. Yose b. R. Bun, "That very night, his cow gave birth to a red heifer [a very rare, valuable specimen suitable for use in the rite of purification described at Num. 19:2-13]. The entire Israelite [nation] paid him [the cow's] weight in gold and bought [the red cow]."
Said R. Yose b. R. Bun, "That very night his cow produced a red heifer and the Israelites paid him its weight in gold and weighed it [for use in producing purification water in line with Num. 19:2 ff.]."	
Said R. Shabbetai, "It is written, 'The Almighty—we cannot find him; he is great in power and justice, and abundant righteousness he will not violate' (Job 37:23)."	Said R. Shabtai [printed editions 3b], "[This story accords with that which] is written [in Scripture, 'Shaddai—we cannot attain to Him]—He is great in power and justice.
The Holy One, blessed be He, will not long delay the reward that is coming to gentiles for the good they do.	And he does not torment those abundant in righteousness' (Job 37:23)—[which means] the Holy One, Blessed be He, does not delay payment to a [righteous] gentile who performs a religious duty [incumbent only upon Israelites]."

The opening of the Jerusalem Talmud story, told by R. Hezekiah, emphasizes that Dama was a gentile and a simple man, specifically in the honor he showed his father. When his father died, he deified him. This detail, which has no link to his negotiation with the Sages, shows that Dama actually worshipped his father. However, the story of the negotiation shows not only Dama's relationship with his father, but his extreme integrity, the more conspicuous because the Sages do not understand it almost until the end of the story, when Dama teaches them a lesson, and almost reprimands them: "Now shall I sell you my father's honor for money?"

The red heifer story is an additional lesson unrelated either to the story per se or to its moral. It comes from a late Amora, R. Yose b. R. Bun, and was added to emphasize again that Dama was a gentile, and that "The Holy One, blessed be He, will not long delay the reward that is coming to gentiles for the good they do."

These, therefore, are different stories told by Eretz Israel Amoraim about the gentile from Ashkelon, Dama bar Nethinah, worked into one account where the protagonist serves as a model in several matters.

In the Babylonian Talmud stories, no dialogues reflect the differences of perception between Dama and the Sages of Israel. There are no different versions

Two things stand out in the Babylonian Talmud: (a) The story is not used to answer the question "How far does honor to parents extend?" but rather as an addendum to others that do answer it. (b) There is additional detail on certain points, detail that is particularly conspicuous against the strong tendency to minimalize in the stories of Dama and his father, and even in some parts of the story of Dama and his mother. It appears that the editor in the Babylonian Talmud did not bring in Dama and his mother to teach how far honor to one's parents extends, but rather to show how such honor is tested in the strained but not uncommon relations between a mother and a son.

The difference between the Jerusalem and the Babylonian stories shows that the Babylonian narrator chose to condense certain aspects and expand others, to emphasize a special point of view. He does not bother with details about Dama son of Nethinah's position, but takes pains to describe the high prestige of Dama son of Nethinah within the situation that was the background for the incident with his mother. The description of her behavior is long, and paints a picture of prolonged suffering and humiliation. By contrast, the son's reaction is given in just two words that succinctly and accurately transmit the narrator's message. The son does not retaliate: she has shamed him and he does not shame her. ("And did not shame her" is linked to R. Eleazer's reply to "How far does honor to parents extend?" His answer was "to throwing a purse into the sea before him, and not shaming him (his father)" (Kidushin 32a). Hence honor to parents extends to situations that demand extreme self-restraint.)

The aspect of shame is emphasized in the Babylonian Talmud. It is not simply losing money, as in the story of Dama and his father, nor of consideration and courtesy, as in other stories in the same Talmudic discussion about Abimi and his father. We are concerned here with the strange, humiliating behavior of the mother and the fact that her son did not react to it. (The Midrash states that she was feeble-minded).

---

as to where the key was, there is no negotiation about a fee, and instead of "jaspis" there is "merchandise" or "gems for the ephod." The negotiators are Sages, not Israel or all Israel.

The Babylonian Talmud appears to have omitted all the details that created a plot, and all messages irrelevant to what the editor considered the only important one—honoring one's father.

The Jerusalem Talmud story centers around the interesting and impressive figure of Dama bar Nethinah, a simple gentile but a scrupulously honest man. He honors his father and his fellow men, takes no advantage of weaknesses, and does not deceive. In the Babylonian Talmud there remains only the condensed story about the honor he gave his father.

In my opinion, the Babylonian Talmud formulation of the story reveals a special way of looking at the relationship of mothers and sons. By contrast, the stories of Dama and his father simply show a one-sided relationship: the father is asleep, taking no part in the narrative, and we have no idea how he treated his son. The honor the son shows his father is emphasized. In the story of Dama and his mother, however, she dominates while he remains passive. In none of the Babylonian Talmud stories about fathers and sons does the father do anything strange, while in all the stories about mothers, of which the Dama bar Nethinah is the first, the mothers are active to the point of hysteria.

Dama's mother knows no limits of due respect or of circumstance, permitting herself a show of authority and exaggerated familiarity in relation to her son at any time and place. The relationship is marked by domineering disrespect on her part, and submission on his. (While the words "and did not shame her" are taken from R. Eleazer's remarks on the limits of honoring one's father, he was talking about a theoretical possibility rather than an actual case. In all concrete cases introduced in the issue, it is the mother's conduct that is domineering.)

This aspect of mother-son relationships finds expression in the group of three stories placed at the end of the Babylonian Talmud discussion now to be examined. Between the second and the third stories in the group there is a saying of R. Johanan and the Gemara's response, formulated as a comparison between that saying and the saying of Abaye. Hence we can conclude that all the elements of the Talmudic passage are taken from different sources and arranged as they are for a specific purpose. After all, R. Johanan, who lived in Eretz Israel, could not have replied to Rav Joseph who lived later in Babylon. Abaye's saying and the discussion based on it were brought together either in or after Abaye's time, which is after the time of Rav Joseph, who was his teacher, and certainly after the time of R. Johanan. Editing has been carried out to link the views of Amoraim who lived in different times and places.

To understand the editorial purpose in the Babylonian Talmud, we begin by examining each story separately and then the arrangement and structure of the entire collection. Since each has a parallel in the Jerusalem Talmud, a helpful comparison can be made between the two.

Some points about these parallels: The first story, about R. Tarfon and his mother, appears both in Kidushin and Peah. The second, about Rav Joseph, has no exact parallel in the Jerusalem Talmud. However, in my opinion it is based on another Eretz Israel story that is placed after that of R. Tarfon in those tractates.

This is the bizarre story of R. Ishmael and his mother, and from the sayings that follow, it is clear beyond doubt that it was deliberately placed after the story of R. Tarfon. The stories complement one another: the one about R. Tarfon tells of a son who is dedicated to his mother's comfort, and the other tells of a mother whose devotion to her son's welfare is unusual to the point of deviance. However, from the morals drawn by R. Mana and R. Zeira, following and linking the stories in the Jerusalem Talmud,[6] one infers that they relate to both parents and not specifically to the mother.

The story of Rav Joseph, the second in the Babylonian Talmud, contains in inverted order the essence of the idea in the Jerusalem

---

[6] Jerusalem Talmud

Kidushin chap. 1, Halakhah 7	Peah chap. 1, Halakhah 1
Said R. Mana, "Well do the millers say, 'Everyone's merit is in his own basket.' [That is there is a different way of doing good for every man (following Pene Moshe & Jastrow).]	Said R. Mana, "The millers have spoken well: 'Each person's merit is within his own basket.'" [That is, each person produced an amount of flour dependent not upon the *amount* of grain he harvests, but upon the *quality* of grain he happens to process. In the present context, this means that the value of Tarfon's and Ishmael's deeds depends not on the amount of respect with which they treated their mothers, but upon their mothers' perceptions of their actions.]
The mother of R. Tarfon said one thing to them, and they responded thus, and the mother of R. Ishmael said something else, and they responded so."	[Thus when] R. Tarfon's mother told them [the aforementioned events, namely, that her son treated her with too much respect, the Sages] replied to her thus, [that he had not treated her with enough respect]. [And when] R. Ishmael's mother told them [the aforementioned events], namely that her son was disrespectful, they replied to him thus [that he must treat her in accord with her wishes, however disgusting he might find them].
R. Zeira was distressed, saying, "Would that I had a father and a mother, whom I might honor, and so inherit the Garden of Eden." When he heard the teachings about Tarfon and Ishmael he said, "Blessed be the All-Merciful, that I have no father and mother. I could not behave like R. Tarfon or R. Ishmael."	Throughout much of his life, R. Zeira was troubled and said, "Would that I had a mother and father, whom I could honor and thereby inherit the Garden of Eden!" [But] when he heard these two stories, he said, "Praise God that I have neither father nor mother; I am not capable of acting like R. Tarfon, nor could I tolerate what R. Ishmael tolerated!"

Talmud story about R. Ishmael. We are not looking at the same story edited or rewritten, but rather a reincarnation, as it were, of a single literary idea.[7] (R. Johanan's saying, "Happy is he who has not seen them," which links the second and third stories in the Babylonian Talmud, has a more developed parallel in R. Zeira's saying, introduced in the Jerusalem Talmud.)

The third story, about Rav Assi and his mother, has no parallel either in Kidushin or Peah in the Jerusalem Talmud, but it does have parallels in three other places, which provide an enlightening comparison.

Let us begin with the first story, as it appears in the Babylonian Talmud:

ר' טרפון הוה ליה ההיא אמא
דכל אימת דהוא בעיא
למיסק לפוריא
גחין וסליק לה
וכל אימת דהוה נחית
נחתת עלויה
אתא וקא משתבח בבי מדרשא
אמרי ליה
עדיין לא הגעת לחצי כיבוד
כלום זרקה ארנקי בפניך לים
ולא הכלמתה?

R. Tarfon had a mother for whom, whenever she wished to mount into bed,
he would bend down to let her ascend
and when she wished to descend she stepped on him.
He went and boasted thereof in the school.
Said they to him,
"You have not yet reached half the honor [due].
Has she thrown a purse into the sea before you without you shaming her?"

And here is the story as it appears in the Jerusalem Talmud:

---

[7]The collection comes in the Babylonian Talmud after Rav Jacob bar Abbuah's question to Abaye about receiving services from one's father and mother, and his answer "From your mother you may receive them, and from your father you may not." The story of R. Ishmael's mother in the Jerusalem Talmud fits in with this question, and is a better basis for stories in the Babylonian Talmud than the one about Rav Jose in the Babylonian Talmud itself.

Mothers and Sons 109

Jerusalem Talmud
Peah chap. 1, Halakhah 7

אמו של רבי טרפון ירדה לטייל
(וטיקן: בחצרה, אין שבת)
הלך רבי טרפון
והניח שתי ידיו
תחת פרסותיה
והיתה מהלכת עליהן
עד שהגיעה למיטתה
פעם אחת חלה ונכנסו חכמים לבקרו

אמרה להן התפללו על טרפון בני
שהוא נוהג בי כבוד יותר מדאי
אמרין לה מה הוא עבד ליך
ותנייית להן עובדא
אמרין לה: אפילו הוא עושה כן
אלף אלפים
עדיין לחצי כיבוד
שאמרה תורה לא הגיע

R. Tarfon's mother went down for a walk in her courtyard on the Sabbath. [Her slipper came off, and she wouldn't retie it because that would be a violation of the Sabbath laws.] R. Tarfon went and placed his two hands under her feet, so that she could walk on them all the way to her couch.

Some time later, [R. Tarfon] became ill and the Sages went to call on him. [His mother] said to them, "Pray for my son Tarfon, for he treats me with too much respect."
They said to her, "What did he do for you?" She told them the foregoing story.
They said to her, "Even if he were to do thus thousands of thousands [of times more] still he would not attain half [the measure] that the Torah commands [for honor of one's mother]."

Jerusalem Talmud
Kidushin chap. 1, Halakhah 1

אמו של רבי טרפון ירדה לטייל
לתוך חצרה בשבת
ונפסק קורדיקון שלה
והלך רבי טרפון
והניח שתי ידיו
תחת פרסותיה
והיתה מהלכת עליהן עד שהגיעה למיטה
פעם אחת נכנסו חכמים לבקרו
אמרה להן התפללו על טרפון בני
שהוא נוהג בי כבוד יותר מדאי
אמרו לה מה עביד ליך?
ותניית להן עובדא
אמרו לה אפי' עושה כן

אלף אלפים

עדיין לחצי כיבוד
שאמרה התורה לא הגיע

The mother of R. Tarfon went down to take a walk in her courtyard on the Sabbath.

Her slipper came off and R. Tarfon went and placed his two hands under the soles of her feet so that she could walk on them until she got to her couch.

One time Sages went to call on him. She said to them, "Pray for my son Tarfon who pays me entirely too much respect."
They said to her, "What does he do for you?"

She repeated the story to them.
They said to her: "Even if he did thus thousands of thousands [of times more], he still would not have paid half the honor of which the Torah has spoken."

In both the Jerusalem and the Babylonian Talmud, the story is told in two parts. I will discuss the differences between the sources for each part separately.

Part 1: The Jerusalem Talmud tells of a single incident: "R. Tarfon's mother went down for a walk in her courtyard on the Sabbath," (though the Vatican manuscript of Peah omits "the Sabbath.") In the Babylonian Talmud the word 'whenever' indicates a routine action. The Jerusalem Talmud tells us that the mother stepped on her son's hands, while in the Babylonian Talmud she stepped on his body.

Part 2 contains three differences. In the Babylonian Talmud's story R. Tarfon boasts in the school, while in the Jerusalem Talmud it is the mother who praises her son, asking his friends to pray for him. In Peah, R. Tarfon becomes ill and his friends come to visit him. (In the Vatican manuscript there is no "became ill," though it does mention that they came in, which may indicate that "became ill" was dropped by accident.) In the Babylonian Talmud it is mere boasting, while in the Jerusalem Talmud it is a reasonable request.

In the Babylonian Talmud the boasting is insignificant, while in the Jerusalem Talmud the mother says that her son gives her "too much honor."

In the Babylonian Talmud, the friends make use of R. Eliezer's words on the extent of honor due even to mentally deranged parents in their reply to R. Tarfon. In the Jerusalem Talmud they simply say that he has not reached half the honor due to his mother according to the Torah, but do not set limits to this honor.

The Jerusalem Talmud story appears to be an original Eretz Israel account of a specific incident in which R. Tarfon helped his mother, who had difficulty in walking. The main point, however, was that it happened on the Sabbath, and that his mother could not possibly walk because she could not fix her sandal then. This is in some doubt, as the Vatican version of Peah does not specify "on the Sabbath." R. Tarfon's illness is mentioned, at least in Peah, thus informing the reader of the fine relationship between R. Tarfon and his mother.

The differences between the two sources show that in the Babylonian Talmud the story was edited to emphasize a specific point that is entirely absent from the original: the power of the mother over her son. The mother uses her son as a footstool when she wants to get on or off her couch. After all, R. Tarfon could have honored his mother by placing a footstool by the couch, even if she was old, as the exegetes Rosh and Rif state. The story, however, emphasizes a physical relationship of stepping on and controlling.

Tractate Avodah Zarah (10b) relates a story about Antoninus and Rabi: Every day he would serve Rabi food and drink. When he wanted to get onto his bed, he would get down on all fours before it and say, "Climb upon me onto the bed." He (Rabi) answered, "It is unseemly to show such contempt for kingship." Antoninus said, "May I be your footstool in the world to come."

This story points unequivocally to two conclusions. First, crouching before a bed to help an elderly person onto it was a familiar service. Secondly, using the back of the crouching individual indicated control and superiority; when done to an equal or a superior it meant contempt.

From the comparison of the Babylonian and Jerusalem Talmuds' stories, and in view of the significance of stepping on another person's back, it becomes clear that the Eretz Israel story of a tender and loving mutual relationship between mother and son becomes one of domination, expressed by stepping on the son's back, in the Babylonian Talmud. Here all elements of the mother's tenderness and love for her son are absent. Her role ends in the first part and consists simply of stepping on her son and making use of him.

The Babylonian Talmud story appears to have created a new story from diverse Eretz Israel materials. One is the account of R. Tarfon and his mother and the other is the custom of getting down on all fours before the bed of old people to help them up. The result was a new story of an old mother physically helpless and mentally ill, who rules over her submissive son through her weakness.

The second story in the Babylonian Talmud collection is that of R. Joseph and his mother: When R. Joseph heard his mother's footsteps, he would say, "I shall rise before the approaching Shechinah."

Here is the story of R. Ishmael as the Jerusalem Talmud tells it:

Kidushin chap. 1, Halakhah 7	Peah chap. 1, Halakhah 1
אמו של רבי ישמעאל באה וקבלה עליו לרבותינו אמרה להן: גערו בישמעאל בני (ליידן – בישמעאל) שאינו נודג בי כבוד באותה שעה נתכרכמו פניהם של רבותינו אמרו: אפשר ר' ישמעאל לא נדג בכבוד אבותיו? אמרו לה: מה עביד ליך? אמרה: כד דו נפק מבית ועדה אנא בעי משנו רינלוי ומשתי מהן	אמו של רבי ישמעאל באת ואמרה וקבלה עליו לרבותינו אמרה: גערו בר' ישמעאל בני שאינו נודג בי כבוד באותה שעה נכרכמו פניהם של רבותינו אמרין: אפשר לית רבי ישמעאל נדג בכבוד אבותיו? אמרו לה מהו עביד ליך? אמרה: כד נפיק מבית ועדא אנא בעא משונה ריגלוי ומשתי מהן
ולא שביק לי אמרו לו: הואיל והוא רצונה הוא כיבודה.	ולא שבק לי אמרין: הואיל והוא רצונה הוא כבודה.

Ishmael's mother came and complained about her son to our sages. She said to them, "Rebuke Ishmael my son, who does not treat me with respect." At that moment our rabbis' faces flushed [with embarrassment].
They thought: "Is it possible that R. Ishmael does not treat his parents with respect?"
They said to her: "What did he do to you?"

"When he left the scholars' meeting place, I wanted to wash his feet and drink the water, but he wouldn't let me" [thereby showing me disrespect]! They said [to Ishmael], "Since this is her wish, this is [what you must do as a mode of] honoring her."

The mother of R. Ishmael went and complained to the rabbis about him. She said, "Rebuke R. Ishmael my son who does not treat me with respect." At that moment our rabbis' faces grew dark.
They said: "Is it possible that R. Ishmael does not pay honor to his parents?" They said to her, "What did he do to you?"
She said, "When he comes home from the council house, I want to wash his feet in water and drink the water, and he does not let me do it."
They said: "Since that is what seems to be the honor she wants for herself, that indeed is just the kind of honor he must pay her."

The Babylonian Talmud story is highly condensed, describing Rav Joseph's relationship with his mother in terms of adoration. Rav Joseph compares his mother to the Shechinah, and his feelings for her are a mixture of love, honor, and awe. Here too the mother's domination is pithily presented, although we get no account of what she does, and have only her son's feelings.

In the foregoing Jerusalem Talmud story as well, adulation is expressed, this time of the mother for the son. While it is not stated in so many words, the reader is unavoidably led to such an impression.

In both the Babylonian and the Jerusalem Talmud stories, there is a link between adulation or adoration, and feet. In the latter, the mother expresses that feeling toward her son when she wants to drink the water in which she washes his feet, and in the former we read of Rav Joseph, who when he heard his mother's footsteps, said, "I rise before the approaching Shechinah," which is adoration explicit. Here, too, possibly the Babylonian Talmud editor used a motif from the Eretz Israel story and carried it to extremes, but reversed the roles. Thus once again, as in the story of R. Tarfon but carried even further, we have a story of a mother whose domination over her son is limitless.

The third story in the collection is the most problematic and the most interesting. My opinion as to its editorial intent is strongly reinforced by comparing the Eretz Israel sources in three places in the Jerusalem Talmud with the Babylonian Talmud's story that follows:

רבי אסי הוה ליה ההיא אמא זקנה
אמרה ליה בעינא תכשיטין

Mothers and Sons

עבד לה
בעינא גברא
נעיין לך
בעינא גברא דשפיר כותך
שבקה ואזל לארעא דישראל
שמע דקא אזלה אבתריה
אתא לקמיה דרבי יוחנן
אמר לו מהו לצאת מארץ לחוצה
א'ל אסור
לקראת אמא מהו
אמר ליה איני יודע
אתרח פורתא
הדר אתא
אמר ליה אסי נתרצית לצאת המקום יחזירך לשלום
אתא לקמיה דרבי אלעזר
אמר ליה חס ושלום
דלמא מרתח רתח
אמר ליה ואם איתא דרתח
לא הוה מברך לך
אדהכי והכי שמע לארונה דקאתי
אמר אי ידעי לא נפקי

R. Assi had an aged mother.
Said she to him, "I want ornaments."
So he made them for her.
"I want a husband"—"I will look out for you."
"I want a husband as handsome as you."
Thereupon he left her and went to Palestine.
On hearing that she was following him
he went to R. Johanan and asked him,
"May I leave Palestine for abroad?"
"It is forbidden," he replied.
"But what if it is to meet my mother?"
"I do not know," he said.
He waited a short time and went before him again.
"Assi," he said, "you have determined to go; [may] the Omnipresent bring you back in peace."
Then he went before R. Eleazar and said to him,
"Perhaps, God forbid, he was angry?"
"What did he say to you?" enquired he.
"The Omnipresent bring you back in peace," was the answer.
"Had he been angry," he rejoined, "he would not have blessed you." Meanwhile he learned that her coffin was coming.
"Had I known," he exclaimed, "I would never have left."

This story also has two parts. The first tells of the strange relationship between Rav Assi and his mother, with more than a hint of her erotic thoughts about him. The only way out is to run away. The second part deals with Rav Assi's wish to leave Eretz Israel to meet his mother who is coming from abroad. Two things are therefore linked by means of the mother "chasing" her son.

The story of Rav Assi who wants to leave Eretz Israel to meet his mother appears in the Jerusalem Talmud in three different places. In Berachot (chap. 3, Halakhah 1) it comes up in relation to "May a Cohen profane himself for his father's or mother's honor (and go beyond the limits of Palestine to see them)?" Thus the Jerusalem Talmud text Berachot (chap. 3, Halakhah 1):

רבי יסא שמע דאתית אימיה לבוצרה
אתא שאל לרבי יוחנן
מהו לצאת
א''ל אם מפני סכנת דרכים, צא.
אי משום כיבוד אב ואם איני יודע (ליידן – אביו ואמו;
וטיקן אם מפני כבוד אביך ואמך)

אטרח עליו (ליידן נוסף: אמ''ל שמואל בר רב יצחק עוד היא צריכה אטרח)
ר' יוחנן אמר אם גמרת לצאת תבוא בשלום
(וטיקן נוסף: ר' שמואל בר רב יצחק עודה היא צריכה לר' יוחנן ואטרח
עליו אמר גמרת לצאת תבוא בשלום שמע ר' אלעזר אמר אין רשוך.גדולה מזו)

> R. Yosse also, on the news of his mother's arrival at Bozzera[8] asked R. Johanan if he might go there.
> The latter replied: "If there is any danger (for his mother and his presence could get her out of it) you should not hesitate; but if it simply for the sake of doing honor to his parents, there might be a doubt on the subject."
> But as R. Yosse persisted, R. Johanan said: "Since thou art decided to go, go and return in peace."

In Sheviyit (chap. 6, Halakhah 2) the status of Bozzera as regards the impurity of gentile lands is discussed in the following story:

רבי יוסי שמע דאתת אימו לבוצרה
שאל לרבי יוחנן מהו לצאת
אמר ליה אם מפני סכנת דרכים צא

---

[8]Bozzera, a city in eastern Transjordan, east of the Bashan Mountains on the southern border of Trabuna, the district whose northern border is Damascus. "Trichuna in the Bozzera district" (Tosephta Shevi'it 4, 11, Jerusalem Talmud Shevi'it 36, C). The city appears to have been the home of the Sages R. Berachiah, R. Hanun, R. Eleazer of Bozzera, R. Tanhum, and others, and had an important Jewish community. Emissaries of the yeshivas, like Resh Lakish and R. Abbahu, visited there to raise money. R. Johanan seems to have seen it as a gentile city and forbade Cohanim to go there.

אם משום כבוד אמך איני יודע
אמר רב שמואל בר רב יצחק
עוד היא צריכה לרבי יוחנן
אטרח עליו ואמר
אם גמרת לצאת תבוא בשלום
שמע רבי לעזר ואמר
אין רשות גדולה מזו.

> R. Yosse heard that his mother had come to Bozzera.
> He asked R. Johanan if he should leave [to meet her].
> He said to him, "If because of the dangers of the journey, go. If for the sake of honoring your mother, I do not know."
> Said R. Samuel bar R. Isaac,
> "The question still lacks [the authority of] R. Johanan."
> He went to him and he said,
> "If you have decided to go, return in peace."
> R. Eleazar heard and said, "There is no higher authority than this."

In Nazir (chap. 7, Halakhah 1) the story comes up as well, again in connection with the question, "What is the law as to a Cohen's contracting corpse uncleanness to pay respect to his father and mother?"

רבי יסא שמע דאתת אימי לבוצרה (ליידן – אימיה)
אתא ושאל לרבי יוחנן מהו לצאת
אמר ליה מפני סכנת דרכים צא
ואם בשביל כבוד אמך איני יודע
אמר רב שמואל בר רב יצחק
עוד היא צריכה
רבי יוחנן
אטרח עליו ואמר
גמרת לצאת תבוא בשלום
שמע רבי לעזר ואמר
אין רשות גדולה מזו.

> R. Yosa heard that his mother was coming to Bozzera.
> He came and asked R. Johanan: "What is the law about going forth [to receive her, even though this requires traversing a gentile land which is unclean]?"
> He said to him: "If it is because of the dangers of the trip [so as to protect her from brigands], go, but if it is in order to pay respect to your mother, I am not sure of the law."
> Said R. Samuel bar R. Isaac: "The question still troubles R. Johanan, even though he said, because Yosa pressured him, 'since you have decided to go forth, may you come back in peace.'"
> R. Eleazar heard and said, "There is no granting of permission greater than this" [granting of his blessing].

All three sources, then, repeat the story with minimal changes. The protagonist is R. Assi (with variant spellings of his name), apparently a

Cohen, who wants to leave Eretz Israel to meet his mother at a place called Bozzera. The theme in each case is leaving Eretz Israel, and the conflict is as to whether the commandment to honor one's mother justifies entering a defiled land. The question that concerns R. Johanan is whether Assi's departure is necessary for her safety or for her honor as a mother. If the latter is the case, R. Johanan does not know whether or not to say that the journey is permitted.

The Berachot version reads "if for the sake of honoring *father* and mother, I do not know." Here it is a matter of honoring parents, not specifically the mother. Nowhere in Jerusalem Talmud sources is mention made of the previous relationship between R. Assi and his mother, nor of what led to their separation, nor of why the mother was coming to Eretz Israel.

The complete similarity of detail in all the Eretz Israel sources, beside the differences between them and the Babylonian Talmud source, shows clearly that the editor of the Babylonian Talmud's story used the Eretz Israel material about the conflict between the commandment to honor one's mother (or parents) and the prohibition against leaving Eretz Israel for a different purpose. He took advantage of the lack of clarity as to R. Assi's reason for leaving and added another story that gave it a background, thus changing its moral. The Babylonian Talmud story to some extent answers the question of why Rav Assi wanted to go abroad to meet his mother. There is a hint of the reason in the background of their separation: Rav Assi ran away to Eretz Israel from the mother who smothered him with her caprices. But her smothering arms have gotten longer as she follows him to Eretz Israel. Perhaps Rav Assi wants to keep her from settling there beside him, thinking that if he goes out to meet her he can persuade her not to do so. It seems that in the Babylonian Talmud's story Rav Assi does not intend either to honor or help his mother, but to keep on running from her. This emerges from another difference between the Eretz Israel and the Babylonian sources. From R. Johanan's answer to Rav Assi in all the Eretz Israel sources, the former appears to know that he wants to go to meet his mother, but does not know whether this is to help her and bring her safely into the country, or to honor her by receiving her suitably. In the Babylonian Talmud source, however, R. Johanan has no idea why Rav Assi wants to leave. This becomes clear only when he gives a negative answer to the latter's question, "May I leave Eretz Israel and go abroad?" And then Rav Assi adds, "What if it is to meet my mother?" The Babylonian source does not even mention honoring one's mother, which seems to indicate the editor's intention to show that Rav Assi's motive is not to honor his mother, and to hint at some other motive.

R. Johanan's final answer too, "If you have determined to go, may the Omnipresent bring you back in peace," in the Babylonian Talmud is different from all the Eretz Israel sources which say, "If you have determined to go, go and return in peace."

The ambiguous "bring you back" in the Babylonian Talmud has caused controversy among commentators. Some say that R. Johanan understood that R. Assi wished to return to Babylon, explaining the words as a wish for a safe return to that place, his former home. Others, however, interpret the words to mean that R. Johanan knew that R. Assi wished to go out to meet his mother and return.[9]

The first interpretation indicates that R. Assi regretted coming to Eretz Israel and wanted to return to Babylon. Such an understanding of the text strengthens the assumption that the Babylonian Talmud editor's intent in reworking the story was to show that Rav Assi left for Eretz Israel to escape from his mother.

The assumption is reinforced by the story's end. "Meanwhile he learned that her coffin was coming. 'Had I known,' he exclaimed, 'I would never have left!'" is not found anywhere in the Jerusalem Talmud. It is certainly possible to interpret "Had I known I would never have left" as R. Assi's regret that he left for Eretz Israel without any reason. That is to say, if I had known she was so soon to die, there would have been no need to run away from her.[10] (Of course it could also be understood simply as regret that he had left his mother to die.)

It appears, then, that the Babylonian Talmud editor added a quite different tale to the nucleus of the story about Rav Assi's wish to leave Eretz Israel to meet his mother. This one centers around the problem of what Rav Assi would do to observe the commandment of honoring one's mother, without becoming trapped in the mad embrace of that domineering parent.

The moral of the story may be that there is a solution to a relationship with an insane parent, which is what Maimonides understood.[11] On the other hand, an opposite lesson may be derived: that

---

[9]Rashi: "You have decided to go: It is likely that he wished to return to Babylonia, his native place. God grant you return in peace to your place." Maharsha: "Rabbi Johanan even doubted that he only wanted to go to meet his mother and come back."

[10]See Rashash who thought that this was Rabad's interpretation of Hilkhot Mamrim, chap. 6, Halakhah 10; Rashash thought that Rav Yose regretted his idea of running away.

[11]Rambam in Hilkhot Mamrim chap. 6, Halakhah 10 says: "He whose father or mother has gone out of their mind tries to treat them according to their wishes, until mercy is granted them. And if he cannot bear their extreme madness he is to leave them and appoint others to take proper care of them." Rabad contradicted him and wrote: "This is not a proper instruction." Ridbaz expounded that the son

a case like R. Assi's has no solution, because his escape ended in tragedy. In any case, a difficult, deranged mother figure has been created deliberately by the editor of the story to teach its moral.

Having compared the individual stories in the Babylonian Talmud with their Eretz Israel sources we may now go on to compare the entire story section in the Jerusalem Talmud discussion with that in the Babylonian Talmud, to discern the differences in the way the two are ordered.

In the Babylonian Talmud, stories about father-son relationships are separated from those about mothers and sons. We have already seen that in the pair of stories about Dama son of Nethinah the story of the mother comes before the story of the father, while in the Babylonian Talmud the story of the mother is an addition to two versions of the story of the father.

After the stories about Dama in the Babylonian Talmud comes the saying of Abimi, and, from his father, two proofs of his son's fine relationship with him. A question to Abaye follows—from whom to accept services, from father or from mother—and the answer makes a distinction between the two. Next is a group of stories dealing only with mothers, linked by the saying of R. Johanan and a report of Abaye, which is similar to it, and together they constitute a sort of interim conclusion.

In the Jerusalem Talmud, after the two stories about Dama bar Nethinah comes the pair about R. Tarfon and R. Ishmael, followed by the morals drawn from them. In conclusion there is a saying that the Babylonian Talmud attributes to R. Abimi about one who fed his father fat chickens yet inherited Gehenna, and another who yoked his father to the millstones and inherited the Garden of Eden, along with other stories exemplifying this point about the relationship between fathers and sons.

The first in the group of stories about mothers in the Babylonian Talmud is that of Dama bar Nethinah, whose mother is depicted as a domineering hysteric, while he is submissive, suffering her outbursts in silence. This opens the way for a presentation of different relationships between mothers and sons, where the common element is unbridled domination of mothers. The editor has arranged these in ascending order: the first tells of a difficult but bearable relationship, the second of one strange to the point of abnormality, and a third where the only way to deal with it is to run away.

---

lets others reprimand his mother and even strike her, which he cannot do himself. According to him, "This is what the son can resort to because the son is too close to his mother, and she is not ashamed before him, which is not so with others."

The first story is about a submissive son and an old and feeble but domineering mother, describing a relationship that has become routine. Possibly the moral is that such a degree of domination is bearable, and that the son should continue to honor his mother nonetheless.

The second in the group of stories about mothers in the Babylonian Talmud is in fact more a testimony than a story, and tells of a relationship that deviates from the norm as regards the son, whose submission to his mother goes beyond anything in our ken. He treats her as the Shechinah; we do not know if her behavior has contributed to this, since nothing she has done is described. The story proposes no escape. However, R. Johanan's saying, "Happy is he who has not seen them," introduced immediately afterward, hints perhaps that the only way out is the mother's early death, which mortal man does not control.

The third story too is about a relationship that is extraordinary to the point of being bizarre, and here the cause is without a doubt the mother's behavior. The son tries to live normally and to honor his mother. She, however, makes insane demands that contain erotic hints, and these force her son to flee from her. The moral of the story is that such a relationship cannot and should not be continued: one is better off escaping from it.

Rav Assi runs from his mother so as not to dishonor her. Possibly the narrator wants to hint that escape here is a necessity, since only thus can the son maintain his honor for his mother.

The way the stories are formulated and arranged seems to highlight a characteristic of mother-son relationships, and to hint at a very delicate balance between the maternal desire to dominate and the submission of sons: if the balance is upset, results may be dangerous and even tragic. If this is indeed the editor's intent, it indicates close and penetrating observation of the emotional and instinctual complexities of motherhood (particularly as regards the mothers of sons), and an awareness and understanding of women's most hidden thoughts.

Afterword

Talmudic literature in general, both law and legend, reflects male points of view. Women are perceived as the second sex, whose appointed roles and purposes are inferior to those of men. Their proper place is at home, and the end and aim of their existence is first of all the welfare of men.

These perceptions and viewpoints are evident in the overt or surface stratum. However, careful examination of individual stories and of collections in which women are the protagonists show different viewpoints, hidden in the deeper layers, between the lines of separate stories and in the seams, as it were, that connect them.

After stating my conclusions from the collections of stories examined, I shall put forward a more general one about the positions of the Sages of the Talmud on women and womanhood.

The design and structure of the collection dealing with "How we dance before the bride" show understanding and sensitivity as regards the world of women. The Sages consider it so important to make the bride feel happy that to achieve this aim they depart from their usual behavior code and act freely, even permissively.

True, the stories express prevailing male perceptions too, like the one that Torah studies should not be interrupted for the sake of a courteous and humane gesture to a woman, that a man should not frolic before her and certainly not touch her physically. At the same time, however, there is sensitivity to the woman's feelings, and the conduct that shows encouragement and human warmth is commended, even if it means overlooking the aforementioned prohibitions.

Various cases are described in the collection dealing with claims of a bride's nonvirginity. When these are investigated, both the individual verdicts and the way the collection is arranged show clearly that the editor intended to show that the letter of the law is essentially a theory: in practice marriages were not annulled because of claims of nonvirginity. Even in extreme cases, where the wife had no chance to bring evidence to disprove her husband's assertions, a way is found to give her legal help and affirm the marriage.

The third collection is about scholars who left home to study Torah. Individual stories were edited to adapt them to their assigned place in the collection, edited in a way that expresses and emphasizes the importance of spiritual partnership and mutual sensitivity between marriage partners. This is placed even above Torah study.

The arrangement of the stories highlights the idea that ignoring the wife's feelings or alienation from her lead inevitably to failure and even calamity. On the other hand, mutual understanding and common purpose can overcome obstacles and bring success.

The fourth collection, on women and wine, indicates clearly how the editor tried to show that whether or not to award a wine allowance to women not living with their husbands was in fact determined by social and economic considerations. This was a departure from the arrogant male perception of women that lay behind the verdict "Wines are not awarded to a woman."

The fifth collection, dealing with relationships between mothers and sons, does not display any particular empathy for women or mothers. In fact, just the opposite is true. The protagonists of these stories are hysterical, insane, and domineering. Paradoxically, however, it is these very stories that show sensitive and penetrating observation of characteristic ways in which women and mothers think and behave.

Careful study of these five collections enables us to perceive with certainty a gap between the clearly male positions expressed in the visible stratum of the stories of the Sages and particularly in the laws, and the consideration for women, the sensitivity toward them, and even the identification with their positions to be found in the hidden strata.

True, neither in the collections nor in the individual stories is there a call to make women and men equal before the law, or even an open appeal for consideration of what women say or desire. However, against the background of that time and place such clear statements from the Sages are not to be expected. We must be content with hints between the lines, which disclose the liberal spirit within the people who arranged the stories and collections.

The most interesting finding in the research on the collections of stories and the Talmudic issues of which they form a part is the gap that existed between the letter of the law and actual practice in matters connected with the status of women. Four of the five collections describe behavior incompatible with what the Halakhah states.

The Halakhah says that men are forbidden to look at the bride's face, and the stories instruct to the contrary.

Afterword

The Halakhah says that a man's claim of his bride's nonvirginity is to be believed, but the stories lead to the opposite conclusion.

The Halakhah allows scholars to leave their homes for long periods to study Torah, while the stories express reservations, making absence conditional on the wife's wishes.

The Halakhah declares that wine allowances are not awarded to women, but the stories reject the prohibition, making the wine allowance a function of economic status.

The discrepancy between the explicit law in the Halakhah and actual practice as portrayed in the stories, exists on many planes in Talmudic literature. Finding this gap as it relates to attitudes toward women shows the existence of advanced and egalitarian trends of thought.

But the examination already carried out is not enough. To reach firm conclusions about the attitude of the Sages toward women and womanhood I shall have to examine other collections and stories, such as the one in Kidushin 82a,b, which deals with ruling one's instincts. Indeed, I intend to start a new study shortly, to deal with stories of women in the Talmud Seder Nashim. In the hope of having the strength to carry out this plan, I pronounce *Women and Womanhood* finished but not complete.

Bibliography

Mishnah, Tosephta, Babylonian Talmud, Jerusalem Talmud, Midrash Rabba, Midrash Hagadol, Aruch

Talmudic Commentaries

Commentary of Rabbenu Hananel in Otzar Hageonim on Ketubot. Levin. Jerusalem, 1939.

Rashi and Tosafot in our printed versions.

Rashi, First Edition according to Commentaries of Rivan, Epstein Edition.

Teshuvot Ha-geonim Harkavi.

Tosafot Yeshanim, Vilna Talmud, Re'em Edition.

Tosafot Rid, Vilna Talmud, Re'em Edition.

Hagahot Ha-Bach, our printed versions.

Maharsha, Hidushei Halakhot ve-Agadot, our printed versions.

Ha-Ran al Ha-Rif, our printed versions.

R. Yehoshua Boaz le-Bet Baruch (Shiltei Giborim) on the Rif, our printed versions.

Tosaphot HaRosh Ha-shalem on Ketubot, according to manuscripts, Shragga Haran Wilman. Tel Aviv, 1973.

Rashba, Tosaphot Rashba on Ketubot.

Ritba, Hidushim on Ketubot.

Hameiri, R. Menahem ben Shlomo le-Bet Meir, Beth Ha-bekhirah, R.A. Sopher. Jerusalem, 1947.

Ran, Shitah le-ha-Ran, from manuscript, Leon Arieh Feldman. Jerusalem, 1956.

R. Joseph Havivah, Nimukei Yosef on Rif. Pressburg, 1838.

Sepher Ravan or Even Ha-ezer, Eliezer ben Nathan. New York, 1958.

Sepher Ha-agudah, Alexander Zuslin Hacohen. Krakow and Jerusalem, 1979.

R. Bezalel Ashkenazi, Shitah Mekubetzet. Tel Aviv, 1965 (Ministry of Religion Edition).

Masekhet Ketubot with alternative versions in Talmudic manuscripts and in Rashi, Rabbi Moshe Hershler, ed. Jerusalem, 1977.

Manuscripts and Printed Versions

A. Manuscripts

The Gemarot Ketubot and Gittin in the Firkovitz Leningrad manuscripts are hereafter marked *LF*.

This manuscript is in the Saltykov-Shchedrin Public Library, and contains the tractates Ketubot and Gittin. It appears to have been written in the early 12th Century, in one of the eastern countries. The first 17 pages of Ketubot are missing, and pages 17b line 31 to 36a line 11 have erasures and blurs that make it possible to read only isolated lines. Hence in chap. 2 and chap. 3, comparisons were not made with this version.

Munich manuscript, hereafter marked *M*.

This manuscript is in the Municipal Library of Munich and is the only one in the world that contains the entire Babylonian Talmud. It was written in the 14th Century, and contains many marginal notes that set forth changed versions. Hence it may be assumed to include versions from several manuscripts.

Manuscript Rome A, hereafter marked *RA*.

This manuscript contains only chap. 1 to 3 of Ketubot, and the beginning of chap. 4, so that it cannot be used in connection with scholars who left their homes, and women and wine. It appears to have been written in the 13th century, and is in the basic collection of the Vatican.

Manuscript Rome B, hereafter marked *RB*.

This contains Ketubot, chap. 1 to 5 and the beginning of chap. 6. It appears to have been written in the 12th century and is in the basic collection of the Vatican.

Manuscript Rome C, hereafter marked *RC*.

This includes the entire tractate Ketubot, and was proofread several times. In its margins are shorthand versions of commentaries, most of which are like Rashi's. It too is in the basic Vatican collection.

Bibliography

Manuscript Rome D, hereafter marked *RD*.
   It contains pages 9b to 100a of Ketubot, with a few missing pages. There are very old versions and proofreading marks, mostly changes of wording. The manuscript is in the basic Vatican collection.

B. Printed Versions

Soncino Press, to be marked *S*.
   It dates from the late 15th century and is in Lombardy. This version served as the basis for subsequent Venice-Bomberg editions.

First Venetian edition, to be marked *V*.
   It dates from 1521 and is in Venice. It was printed from a manuscript and from the Soncino printing.

Agadot Hazal in the Paris manuscript, to be marked *HP*.
   The collection is in the National Library in Paris, and contains collections of stories from Kidushin, Ketubot, Sotah, Gittin, and Hulin.

Agadot Ha-Talmud, Constantinople manuscript, to be marked *H1*.
   It contains all the stories of the Talmud and was printed in Constantinople in 1515.

Agadot Hazal, Parma manuscript, to be marked *H2*.
   The collection is in the libary at Parma, and contains an ancient copy of Hagadot Ha-Talmud, printed in Constantinople in 1511, and apparently written in Spain.

Agadot Ha-Talmud, British Museum version, to be marked *H3*.
   The collection is in the British Museum Library in London. It appears to be a later copy of the Constantinople version.

Ein Ya'akov, to be marked *E*.
   Contains all the stories from the Talmud, in order of the tractates in which they appear, printed in 1516 in Saloniki.

C. Geniza Fragments of Ketubot

In *Talmud Bavli im Dikdukei Sofrim ha-Shalem*, Gemara fragments from the Geniza have been arranged according to the form of the script, the order, the tradition of reading and pointing, and correspondence to 48 units, each one marked with the letter 'ג, and a number in a series. The units related to the chapters in this book are:

47'ג – This unit is in Melk, Austria, and contains pages 10b to 11a.

59'ג – This unit is in Cambridge, England, and contains pages 62b to 63a.

Books and Articles in Hebrew

Albeck, Hanoch. *Mehkarim be-Beraita ve-Tosephta ve-yahasan le-Talmud*. Jerusalem, 1944.

Allon, Menahem. *Ha-mishpat Ha-Ivri*. Jerusalem, 1973.

Aminoach, Noah. *Masekhet Kidushin*. Tel Aviv, 1987.

Barron, Shalom. *Historiah Hevratit ve-Datit shel Am Israel*. Tel Aviv, 1956-1957.

Ber, Moshe. *Amorayei Bavel, Prakim be-Hayei Khalkhalah*. Ramat Gan, 1965.

Berkovitz, Eliezer. "Ma'amad ha-Ishah be-Yahadut, Hebet Halakhati Hevrati." *Hagut, Me'aseph l'Machashavah Yehudit*. Jerusalem, 1983.

Draizin, Nahum. "Ma'amadan ve-Hinukhan shel Nashim be-Halakhah." *Or Ha-mizrah* 16, (1967).

Elbaum Ya'akov. "Demuyot Nashim be-Agadot Hazal – Model le-Hikui." *Hagut, Me'aseph le-Mahashavah ha-Yehudit*. Jerusalem, 1983.

Elitzur, Yehuda. "Ha-Ishah be-Mahashevet ha-mikra." In *Hagut, Me'aseph le-Mahashavah ha-Yehudit*. Jerusalem, 1983.

Feldman. *Tsimhei Ha-Mishnah: Tiuram Ha-botani ve-Erkham ha-Khalkhali be-Avar u-va-Hoveh*. Tel Aviv, 1962.

Frankel, Yonah. *Iyunim be-Olamo ha-Ruchani shel Sippur ha-Agadah*. Tel Aviv, 1981.

Friedman, Shamma. *A Critical Study of Yevamot with a Methodological Introduction*. New York, 1978.

Ginsburg, Levi. *Pirushim ve-Hidushim be-Yerushalmi*. New York, 1941.

Halivni (Weiss), David. *Mekorot ve-Masorot, Bi'urim be-Talmud, Seder Nashim*. Tel Aviv, 1968.

Halevi, A.A. *Agadah ve-Halachah le-Or Mekorot Yevaniim ve-Latiniim*. Tel Aviv, 1980.

Hebrew Encyclopedia, s.v. "hatunah."

Heimann, A. *Toldot Tanna'im ve-Amora'im*. Jerusalem, 1964.

Herschberg. *Hayei ha-Tarbut be-Israel be-Tekufat ha-Mishnah ve-ha-Talmud*. Warsaw, 1924.

Hildesheimer, Azriel. "Toldot Berachot Erusim ve-Nesuim." *Sinai*, 10.

Jacobs, I.L. "Ha-Hayim ha-Khalkhaliim shel Yehudei Bavel be-Tekufat ha-Talmud." *Melilah*, 5.

Klein, Shmuel. *Eretz Israel me-Yemei ha-Aliyah me-Bavel ad Hatimat ha-Talmud*, Jerusalem, 1966.

Kosovsky, Haim Yehoshua. *Otzar Leshon ha-Talmud*. Jerusalem, 1960-1962.

Levin, Benyamin Menashe. *Rabbanan Sevoraei ve-Talmudam*. Jerusalem, 1929.

Liebermann, Shaul. *Al Hayerushalmi*. Jerusalem, 1929.

———.*Tosephta ke-Peshuta, Seder Nashim*. New York, 1967.

Ne'eman, Pinhas. *Encyclopedia of Talmudic Geography*. Tel Aviv, 1970-1971.

Ozick, Cynthia. "He'arot le-shem Metziat ha-She'elah ha-Nekhonah. *Ha-Peninah*. Jerusalem, 1983.

Pinelish, Hirsch Mendel. *Darchah shel Torah*. Vienna, 1861.

Rabenu, Nathan me-Romi. *Ha'aruch Hashalem*. New York 1956.

Rabinovitch, Z. *Sha'arei Torat Eretz Israel*. Jerusalem, 1940.

Silberg, Moshe. *Ha-Ma'amad ha-Ishi be-Israel*. Jerusalem, 1958.

Supreme Court Judgments in Israel. Vol. 42, pp. 221-277.

Weiss, Abraham. *Al ha-Yitzirah ha-Sifrutit shel ha-Amoraim*. New York, 1962.

———. *Le-Heker ha-Talmud*. New York, 1955.

———. *Hithavut ha-Talmud be-Shlemuto*. New York, 1943.

Zimmerman, David. *Shemonah Sippuri Ahava min ha-Talmud ve-ha-Midrash*. Tel Aviv, 1981.

Books and Articles in English

Amado Levy Valency, Eliana. "Civilizations and their Attitudes Towards Women." *Prooftext* 10.

Boyarin, Daniel. "Internal Opposition in Talmudic Literature." *Presentation* 36. Berkeley, 1991.

———. *Carnal Israel*. Berkeley, 1993.

Encyclopedia Judaica, s.v. "marriage," "virginity," "wine."

Friedman, Theodore. "The Shifting Role of Women from the Bible to the Talmud." *Judaism* 36, 4, 1987.

Greenberg, Blu. *On Women and Judaism: A View from Tradition*. Philadelphia, 1981.

Ilan, Tal. *Jewish Women in Graeco-Roman Palestine*. Tübingen, 1995.

Neusner, Jacob. *The Jerusalem Talmud.* Chapter 6 (Kidushin and Peah). Chicago.

Preuss, Julius. *Biblical and Talmudic Medicine.* New York and London, 1978.

Schwab, Moses. *The Jerusalem Talmud.* (Berachot) New York.

Index of Texts Discussed

Bible

Genesis
24:60 11
2:22 24

Numbers
19:2-13 104

Deuteronomy
22:22 viii
11:19 xii
22:23-27 29
22:13-22 29

Judges
6:21 24
21:12 45

1 Samuel
1:9 .... 86, 89

Isaiah
57:21 19
27:22 30

Zephaniah
3:13 36

Psalms
65 85

Job
40:4 20
37:23 104

Ruth
4:11 11

Lamentations
2:13 30

Mishnah and Tosefta

Succah
3:2 20

Moed Katan
2:1 20

M. Ketubot
4:3 30
1:2 30
1:1 31
1:5 31
1:6 31
1:7 31
5:8 81

T. Ketubot
5:7 80-81

M. Kiddushin
3:10 35

Niddah
9:11 46

Shevi'it
6:2 114

Babylonian Talmud

Berachot
57a 20
35b 77
63a 87
42b 95
57a 99

Eruvin
100b x
64b 77

Shabbat
133b 2
116a 16
33a 94

Pesahim
106a 2
107a 77

Yoma
73b 16
78a 66

Ta'anit
29b 44
27a 96
18a 85

Moed Katan
28b 2
25a 23

Hagigah
14a 16

Yevamot
63a-63b .... xi, xii
107a 37
60b 45
65b 66
64b 93

Ketubot
16b-17a 11, 12, 21
7b-8a 11
62b 23
77b 23
8a-9a 32
8b-10b 32
9a 33, 34
15a 34
10b 44
62b-63a 51
61b-62a 53
103a 62
64b-65a 77
64a 78
64b-65a 79

Nedarim
50a 71
49b 77

Nazir
7b 23

Index of Texts Discussed

Sotah
2a 78-87

Kidushin
29b xii
71a 23
45b 36
30b-31a 99, 100, 102
32a 105
82a-82b 123

Baba Kama
71a 20

Baba Mezia
44b 65

Baba Batra
59a 70
58b 77
12b 77
60b 78

Sanhedrin
4b 2
38b 2
70a 78
70b 78

Avodah Zarah
23a-24b 102
10b 110

Avot d'Rabbi Nathan
4:2 .... 18, 19, 26
6 (13 13) 72, 86

Tractate Kallah
1 11

Kallah Rabbati
9 13
2:8 87

Derech Eretz Rabbati
6 13

Niddah
64b 47
8b 47

Jerusalem Talmud

Berachot
3:1 114

Peah
1:1 .... 19, 20, 21, 99, 100,
   .... 103, 107, 109, 111

Shevi'it
6:2 114

Ma'aser sheni
4:6 88

Bikkurim
2:3 63

Pesachim
3:7 74

Taanit
4:2 65
4:3 65

Hagigah
1:7 .... 19, 74

Ketubot
1:1 .... 30, 32, 46

5:11 81
11:1 92

Nazir
7:1 115

Kidushin
1:7 .... 99, 100, 103,
.... 107, 109, 111

Baba Mesia
4:1 63

Avodah Zarah
3:1 ....19, 21

Midrash
Bereshit Rabbah 16, 21,
.... 65, 67
Vayikra Rabbah 67
Devarim Rabbah.............100
Aichah Rabbati 81
Tanhuma 88
Yalkit Shimoni 2, 88
Midrash Hagadol............. 18

Index of Names

A
Abaye, 85, 86, 89, 90, 91, 93, 94, 106, 118
Abbahu, 14-16, 81, 82, 85
Abimi, 105, 118
Adda bar Ahavah, 53, 56
Aha, 17, 24, 25, 27
Ahai, 40, 42
Akiva, 62, 68
Ammi, 14, 16
Ashi, 44
Assi, 14, 16, 108, 113-119

B
Ben Kalba Savu'a, 61, 71
Berekhah, 2
Beth Hillel, 13-15, 18, 25
Beth Shammai, 13-15, 18, 25
Brona, 56

D
Dama son of Nethina, 99-102, 105, 106, 118
Dimi, x, 14, 15, 16, 100

E
Eleazar, xi, 32-37, 82, 84, 85, 89, 91, 97, 113, 115
Eliezer, 53, 55, 56, 71, 73, 100, 101, 110, 126

H
Hama, 54, 60, 69, 70, 74, 76
Hama bar Bisa, 54, 60, 69, 70, 73, 76
Hananyah ben Hakhinai, 59
Hanina, 47, 59, 67-70
Hannah, 84-87, 89
Hezekiah, 66, 81-82, 90, 101
Hila, 31
Hinena b. Kahana, 84
Hisda's daughter, 93
Hiyya, xi, 53, 54, 57, 58, 63-66, 75, 81-82
Hiyya bar Adda, 81-82
Huna, 44, 54, 57, 77, 85
Huna Mar son of Rava of Parazkia, 44

I
Isaac son of Joseph, 17, 19, 21, 22, 23, 24, 26, 27, 94, 115
Ishmael, 80, 102-108, 111-112, 118

J
Jannai, 57, 63, 64, 66
Jeremiah b. Abba, 47
Johanan, 81, 83, 85, 101, 106, 108, 113, 115, 119

Jonathan, 14, 25, 26, 66
Jose, xii, 47, 80
Jose bar Abin, 47
Joseph, 36, 63, 94-96, 100, 106, 108, 111, 113, 125
Joshua, 71, 73, 78, 81, 82, 94
Josi, 65, 66
Judah, 3, 11, 17-19, 24, 26-27, 34, 46, 52-54, 57, 63-66, 75, 72, 84-85, 89, 91, 101-102
Judah bar Ila'I, 17-19, 24, 26-27
Judah of Kfar Nabirya, 84-85, 89, 91
Judah the son of Rabbi Hiyya, 53, 57

K
Kahana, 78, 84, 86

M
Mana, 107
Martha daughter of Beithos, 81, 83, 85, 90, 92

N
Nahman, 36, 38-42, 54, 57
Nakdimon ben Gurion's daughter, 85, 86, 90, 91
Nehemiah the son of Rav Joseph, 95

O
Oshaya, 60

R
Rabban Gamaliel, 39, 41-47
Rabban Gamaliel the Elder, 38, 46
Rabban Gamaliel the son of Rabbi, 43-45
Rabbi, xi, xii, 2, 3, 14, 18-19, 26, 38, 39, 43-48, 54, 56-60, 62-63, 65-66, 68-69, 72, 74, 75, 126
Rabbi Judah, 3, 57, 63
Rami bar Hama, 60, 70
Rashi, 33-34, 53, 63, 77, 94, 125-126
Rav, x, xi, 15, 19, 21-24, 39, 40-42, 44, 53-54, 56-57, 63-65, 77, 78, 86, 95, 100-102, 106, 108, 112-114, 116-112, 119
Rav Judah, 11, 54, 57, 77, 101, 103
Rava, 44, 53, 54, 56, 63, 75, 78, 85, 87, 89, 93-95
Rehumi, 52-54, 56, 63-65, 74, 75

S
Samuel, 17, 19, 21, 22, 23, 24, 26, 27, 32-34, 36, 37, 39, 53, 54, 57, 84, 86, 87, 89-91, 101, 102, 115
Samuel the son of Rabbi Isaac, 17
Shefatyah son of Avital, 58
Shimei brother of David, 58
Shimon ben Yohai, 59
Simon son of Eleazar, 36

T
Tarfon, 106-112, 118

U
Ulla, 99, 101, 103

Y
Yosa, 115
Yosef, 63, 125

Z
Zeira, 14-17, 22, 23, 107, 109

Index of Subjects

A
adultery, viii, 30
Amoraim, 3-6, 27, 32, 37-39, 47, 54, 78, 106, 129
annul a marriage, 31
Assyrian law, 29
attitude toward women, xiii, xiv, 3, 123

B
Babylonian Talmud, x, xi, 2-5, 11, 14, 18, 20-24, 29, 32, 35, 36, 51, 63-69, 79, 81, 83, 87, 89, 91, 92, 97, 99, 101, 102, 105, 106, 108, 112, 116, 119, 125, 126
beraita (beraitot), 3, 4, 13, 14, 25, 77, 80, 81, 83, 86, 87, 89, 91
betrothed, 29, 30, 35, 61, 70, 71
bride, 7, 11-21, 24-27, 29, 32, 33, 121-123

C
collection, xi, 2, 4-9, 12, 13, 15, 16, 18-20, 24-26, 33, 37-39, 42, 43, 47, 48, 52-54, 65, 67, 69, 70, 74, 75, 79, 82, 83, 92, 97, 106, 111, 112, 121, 123, 126, 127
conjugal life, 12, 74

D
death by stoning, 29, 30
discriminated, vii, x
discrimination, vii, viii, x, xii
discussion, 4, 6, 8, 9, 12, 14, 18, 25, 32-40, 43, 51-53, 63, 66, 71, 79, 82, 83, 87, 89, 93, 96, 97, 105, 106
Dorkati, 33, 38, 46, 47

E
editing, 2-4, 6, 20, 26, 39, 50, 54, 63
editor, 2, 3, 5, 13, 14, 16, 18, 19, 20, 24, 26, 37, 39, 42, 43, 47, 48, 50, 52, 53, 54, 63, 70, 82, 97, 98, 99, 105, 112, 116-119, 121, 122

F
family, ix, x, xi, 11, 33, 38, 46, 47, 51, 58, 63, 69-71, 74, 75, 77
female, ix-xvi, 2, 7, 9, 37
feminine point of view, 8, 9
feminine position, 7

G
Gemara, 30, 31, 33-37, 39, 40, 43, 45, 47, 55, 66, 67, 77, 89, 90, 92, 106, 127

137

Greek, xii-xiv, 12, 46, 78
Greek culture, xii-xiv
groom, 11

H

Halakha, 19
Halakhic, x, xiii, 4, 8, 9
Halakhic attitude, x
Hittite law, 29

J

Jerusalem Talmud, 2, 3, 19, 21-23, 30-32, 34, 35, 37, 63-65, 79, 81-83, 87, 90-92, 94, 97, 99-102, 106-112, 114, 116-118, 125, 130

L

leaving home, 8, 75
legal status, 8

M

male orientation, vii, xi
marital duty, 51, 52, 54, 63, 64, 66, 75
marriage, xiii, xiv, 7, 8, 14, 29, 31, 32, 51, 52, 54, 65, 66, 68, 70, 73, 76, 94, 96, 122
mothers and sons, 9, 99, 106, 111, 113, 122

O

open, 31-34, 36-43, 48, 49, 78, 122
opening, xii, 31-34, 36-43, 48, 49, 53, 77, 91

P

pillar of fire, 17, 22, 23, 25, 52, 57, 63, 64
position of women, xv
precedent, 44-46

priest, 35

R

rape, viii

S

safek sotah, 30, 31
saying, 25, 36, 38, 56, 61, 69, 71, 73, 74, 78, 82, 90, 106, 108, 118, 119
scholars, vii, x, xiii, xvi, 4, 5, 8, 14-16, 51-54, 57, 112, 122, 123, 126
sex, viii, x, xi, xiii, xvi, 50, 87, 97, 121
sexual behavior, 87
shame, 17, 21, 23, 37, 100, 102, 105, 106
social status, vii, viii, x, xiv, 13
stories, x, xi, 2, 3, 6-9, 12, 13, 18, 19, 23-26, 33, 37-39, 43, 46, 48-54, 63-66, 70, 74-76, 79, 82, 83, 90, 92, 96-103, 105, 108, 111, 112, 118, 123, 127
suspected betrayal, 32, 34

T

Tannaim, 4, 6, 30, 38
Tannaitic, 30, 89, 97
Tannaitic sources, 30

V

versions, xiv, 2, 14, 20, 24, 26, 38, 41, 55, 67, 71, 73, 74, 100, 102, 118, 125, 127
virginal blood, 33, 46
virginity, 7, 8, 29-35, 37, 46-50, 121, 123

Index of Subjects

W

warning and seclusion, 30, 32, 34, 36

wedding celebration, 11-13, 26

whore, 29, 30

widows, 79, 89, 96

wife of, 8, 34, 35, 68, 69, 74, 93, 95, 96

wine, 8, 45-47, 77-97, 122, 123, 128

wine allowance, 8, 79, 81, 82, 86, 87, 89, 90, 93, 97, 122, 123

woman, viii-xiii, xv, 2, 7, 8, 11, 13, 18, 26, 27, 29-36, 45-49, 58, 59, 65, 68, 78, 81, 84, 85, 87, 89-91, 94, 97, 121, 122

women, vii-xvi, 2, 3, 5, 6, 8, 9, 12-15, 26, 27, 30, 33, 37, 46, 49, 51, 53, 68, 76, 78, 81, 83, 85-97, 119, 121, 123, 126

women's status, viii-xv, 3

www.ingramcontent.com/pod-product-compliance
Lightning Source LLC
Chambersburg PA
CBHW030141170426
43199CB00008B/157